TERRORISM FACTBOOK
OUR NATION AT WAR

Thanking Our Heroes

A DEDICATION AND A PROMISE

Oftentimes in the wake of devastating circumstances it takes us months to understand, to cope, and if we're fortunate, years, perhaps even decades later, we may come to terms with the pain and begin again with renewed strength. Indeed, what transpired on September 11 has left us all shuffling through a haze of sadness and loss. 7 out of 10 Americans are suffering from depression. Families all over the world are ravaged. But something sets September 11 apart from other, similarly devastating events in our lives. Yes, the Pentagon/World Trade Center tragedy was the most catastrophic event of terror ever to occur in America, but what sets September 11 apart is that we all evolved that day. And we didn't evolve over the course of 6 months or 5 years, we evolved the moment we saw what happened. Here's why:

The utterly incredible people, the kind of people that most of us have never known before, the people that chose to preserve the lives of individuals that they had never met. Remarkable. Most of us are dubious about whether or not we would have run up the stairs of the World Trade Center, leaving behind our little boys, and our little girls. But if our daughter, all grown up, was working in the Pentagon that day, we would pray to God or Allah that one of those people was there, to run in, pick her up and carry her away from the terror and the flames. And they were there. Hundreds of them. Who would have ever thought that in the early, awestruck moments of such overwhelming catastrophy and dread, when cogent thought is preempted by panic, that America and the World could look on and say with absolute, unwavering confidence that people are basically good.

The publisher of this book would like to thank those people, not simply for saving lives, sacrifice, but for granting all of us clarity in the midst of unspeakable pain. In your final moments you changed the lives of millions of people. Nobody missed it. People spoke of it only moments after the attacks. You showed us that people are good and not only that, people are capable of great things. Now all of us sit at home and in our offices and think: maybe I do have it in me, maybe I would have gone to the front of that plane and taken control away from the hijackers, maybe I'll do something great someday.

And now, here we are, evolved. Humbled. Stronger. Great. We enter into this war with these qualities, deeply ingrained in our countenance. We look at each other and we see it in the eyes of our husbands and wives, we see it in the stoic expression of the clerk at the grocery store. And there is no way any of us will ever let that go. With it we will move forward, stronger, braver and ready to win. In your names, we will fight this battle and with your super human examples of humanity, we will end this terror, forever.

TERRORISM FACTBOOK

MARC MILLER AND JASON FILE

Written and Researched by: Marc Miller and Jason File
Additional Writing and Research: Staley Krause
Graphic Design and Layout: Keith Warren

Many of the maps in this work were contributed by the
Perry-Castañeda Map Collection at the University of Texas, Austin.

Cover Photo: Todd Rengel

Acknowledgements:

Marc Miller dedicates his work on this book to family. If we thought we understood the meaning of
family before, then we understood it much more clearly after September 11. As we drew closer to our own
families, we felt deeply for the thousands of families so tragically affected on that horrible day.
May those who have suffered loss of family find the strength to go on, and those who died,
not have died in vain. To my own family, I thank God for you.

When justice is done, it brings joy to the righteous but terror to evildoers.
– *Proverbs 21:15 - New International Version (NIV)*

Jason File dedicates his work on this book to the victims of the September 11 attacks and their families,
to the rescue workers for their tireless devotion, and to his loved ones, Barbara, Dan, Ben, Louise and Polly.
He would also like to thank the U.S. National Science Foundation, British ORS Scholarships, and
New College, Oxford for financial support of academic work which contributed in part to the contents
of this book, Oxford University Professor Guy S. Goodwin-Gill for supervision,
and the Yale Law School Class of 2004 for support.

The publisher has pledged to donate 10% of sales to the Red Cross Disaster Relief Fund.
For more information about the Red Cross Disaster Relief Fund,
contact 1-800 HELP NOW or visit: http://store.yahoo.com/redcross-wtc1/.

TERRORISM FACTBOOK
OUR NATION AT WAR

Copyright ©2001 Bollix Books

1 2 3 4 5

ISBN: 1-55878-301-6

1609 West Callender Ave.
Peoria, Il 61606
309-676-6558

TABLE OF CONTENTS

MORE THAN AN ACT OF WAR

INTRODUCTION

Soon after the devastating attacks on the World Trade Center and the Pentagon on Tuesday, September 11, 2001, President George W. Bush decried them collectively as 'an act of war.' Cabinet members, legislators, and media commentators quickly joined in this sentiment as America simultaneously mourned the destruction and loss of lives while bristling in preparation for military responses.

Yet if one considers precisely the nature of those attacks, particularly the obliteration of the World Trade Center, it becomes clear that they went beyond our general notion of an act of war. Indeed, if they were committed in the course of a military conflict, they undoubtedly would be deemed a 'war crime.' International law prohibits intentionally targeting innocent civilians during wartime, and dictates that those who plan and carry out such actions are enemies of mankind who should be prosecuted and punished regardless of where in the world they might be found.

Some of these laws of war were codified by the international community in the Geneva Conventions following World War II. But as times have changed, the world has been forced to adapt to evolving techniques of modern warfare. Recent events force us to inquire: what happens in cases like the World Trade Center attack, when such actions occur during what is ostensibly peacetime? Or when they are perpetrated not by uniformed soldiers, but by casually-dressed private civilians who may or may not have a tenuous connection to foreign governments? Such are a few of the many complexities posed by the problem of terrorism which are changing the face of military conflict and

> If one considers the nature of those attacks, particularly the obliteration of the World Trade Center, it becomes clear that they went beyond our general notion of an act of war. Indeed, if they were committed in the course of a military conflict, they undoubtedly would be deemed a 'war crime.'

national security concerns in the 21st century.

This book offers the reader a general introduction to international terrorism and affords an understanding of the events of September 11, 2001 within a broader context than can be gleaned from national news media coverage. In what follows, we investigate controversies involving how to conceptualize terrorism, how to prevent and respond to terrorism, and how to explain why America is a target of terrorism. We consider U.S. policies and international relations which historically have provoked terrorist attacks while also developing profiles of terrorist groups and leaders such as Osama bin Laden. We also highlight the complex relationships between private terrorist groups and states which tacitly or explicitly support them, and what bearing these relationships have on the types of international responses to terrorism which are available under such circumstances.

While this book is not a comprehensive analysis of the entire field of international terrorism, it helps the reader access the most important and relevant issues and understand the depth of the new challenges facing U.S. and world security.

TIMETABLE FOR NOTABLE TERRORIST ATTACKS

* = Attack associated with Osama bin Laden.

*September 11, 2001 -

Terrorists on an organized suicide mission hijack four civilian airliners virtually simultaneously from different airports. After commandeering the flights, the hijackers fly two airplanes into the World Trade Center in New York City, both towers of which collapse after catching fire, killing over 5,000. The third flight strikes the south side of the Pentagon in Washington, D.C., which catches fire, killing almost 200. The fourth flight crashes into the ground in Pennsylvania, on course for Washington, D.C., after an apparent struggle for control of the plane, killing 45.

*October 12, 2000 -

Suicide bombers with explosives on a small boat cripple the destroyer USS Cole in the port city of Aden, Yemen, killing 17 sailors and injuring 39.

*August 7, 1998 -

Suicide bombers driving cars laden with explosives simultaneously destroy the U.S. embassy in Nairobi, Kenya, killing 291 and wounding over 5,000 and the U.S. embassy in Dar es Salaam, Tanzania, killing 10 and injuring 77.

July 27, 1996 -

A pipe bomb explodes in Atlanta during the Olympics, killing one person and wounding 11.

*June 25, 1996 -

A bomb aboard a fuel truck explodes outside a U.S. air force installation in Dhahran, Saudi Arabia. 19 U.S. military personnel are killed in the Khubar Towers housing facility, and 515 are wounded, including 240 Americans.

*November 13, 1995 -

A car bomb in Riyadh, Saudi Arabia kills seven, including five Americans.

April 19, 1995 -

A truck bomb destroys the Murrah Federal Building in Oklahoma City, killing 168 people.

*October 3 and 4, 1993 -

Al Qaeda-trained fighters shoot down two U.S. helicopters in Somalia and kill 18 U.S. soldiers.

*February 26, 1993 -

A bomb in a van explodes in the basement parking garage of the World Trade Center, killing six and injuring 1,042.

December 21, 1988 -

A bomb destroys Pan Am Flight 103 en route from London to New York over Lockerbie, Scotland, killing all 259 people on board, including 189 Americans, and 11 people on the ground.

April 5, 1986 -

A bomb destroys the La Belle discotheque in West Berlin, killing three U.S. soldiers, wounding 80, and injuring over 200 German civilians.

April 2, 1986 -

An explosion blows a hole in the fuselage of TWA Flight 840 from Rome to Athens as it prepares to land. Four of the 114 passengers are sucked out of the aircraft and killed.

December 27, 1985 -

Simultaneous suicide bombings are carried out against U.S. and Israeli check-in desks at Rome and Vienna international airports, killing 20.

November 23, 1985 -

Hijackers aboard an Egyptair flight kill one American. The plane is diverted to Malta, where Egyptian commandos storm the plane. The hijackers detonate several hand grenades. 58 of 90 passengers are killed, along with two of the six crew.

October 7, 1985 -
Palestinian terrorists hijack the cruise liner Achille Lauro. Leon Klinghoffer, an elderly, paraplegic American, is killed and thrown overboard.

August 8, 1985 -
A car bomb at a U.S. Air Force base in Frankfurt, Germany kills two and injures 20. A U.S. airman murdered for his identity papers is found a day after the explosion.

June 6, 1985 -
A TWA Boeing 727 traveling from Athens to Rome is hijacked by two Hezb'allah terrorists and forced to fly to Beirut. The crew and passengers are held hostage for 17 days, which includes two flights to Algiers, Algeria, and the murder of one American. The US pressures Israel to meet the hijackers' demands, and 435 Lebanese and Palestinian prisoners are released from prison. The hostages are then released in Syria after being hidden in various parts of Beirut.

September 20, 1984 -
A Hezb'allah suicide bomber at the US Embassy in Beirut kills 23 and injures 21.

April 12, 1984 -
Hezb'allah bomb kills 18 U.S. soldiers and injures 83 at the U.S. Air Force base in Torrejon, Spain.

October 23, 1983 -
Simultaneous suicide truck bombs by Islamic Jihad on American and French compounds in Beirut destroy U.S. Marine Corps barracks, killing two hundred and forty one Americans, and destroy a French building, killing 50. The U.S. and France respond with air strikes against suspected terrorist camps in the Beka'a Valley.

September 23, 1983 -
An Omani Gulf Airbus traveling from Karachi, Pakistan to Abu Zabi, United Arab Emirates is brought down by a bomb, killing 111 people

April 18, 1983 -
A suicide truck bomb by Islamic Jihad on the U.S. Embassy in Beirut kills 63 and injures 120.

November 4, 1979 -
Extremist Iranian students seize The U.S. Embassy in Tehran, taking 66 U.S. staff and diplomats hostage. The crisis is not resolved until January 20, 1981.

March 11, 1978 -
A landing party of 9 Fatah terrorists come ashore in Israel and hijack a tourist bus on a coastal highway, killing 26 and wounding 70. The terrorists are killed in a gunbattle with Israeli forces; Israel later retaliates by invading Lebanon.

September 10, 1976 -
Croatian terrorists hijack a TWA airliner flying from New York to Paris, seizing 93 hostages. Although the hostages are released later, one New York City police officer is killed by a bomb left in a Grand Central Station locker by the terrorists.

September 5, 1972 -
The Black September terrorist organization executes the Munich Olympic Massacre of eleven Israeli atheletes.

September 6, 1970 -
Members of the Popular Front for the Liberation of Palestine (PFLP) hijack four airliners simultaneously from different airports. The events that transpire ultimately result in the release of six Palestinian Fedayeen extremists from Swiss and German prisons and will come to be known in fundamentalist Islamic groups as 'Black September.'

SEPTEMBER: A SACRED MONTH OF REVOLUTION

Following the September 11, 2001 attacks on the World Trade Center and the Pentagon, discussions in the media described a 'new face of terrorism' while simultaneously expressing frustration at the difficulty in assigning responsibility for the attacks. Yet an eerily similar event over thirty years earlier casts doubt on the novelty of the tactics employed and points to possible terrorist motivations in the more recent disaster.

On September 6, 1970, members of the Popular Front for the Liberation of Palestine (PFLP) hijacked four airliners simultaneously from different airports. Three of the four hijackings were successful, and consisted of a TWA Boeing 707, a SwissAir DC 8, and a PanAm Boeing 747. In the fourth airplane, the passengers and crew managed to overpower the two hijackers, one of whom was killed; the plane was diverted to the nearest airport, London Heathrow, and the remaining hijacker, Leila Khaled, was arrested by British authorities. The TWA and SwissAir flights were forced to land at a desert airstrip near Zarqa, Jordan (15 miles north of Amman). The PanAm 747 was diverted to Cairo, where the hijackers released the passengers and crew, destroyed the airplane with high-explosives, and escaped.

Holding the TWA and SwissAir passengers and crew hostage, the PFLP terrorists demanded the release of six Palestinian Fedayeen extremists who were in Swiss and West German prisons, as well as Ms. Khaled, who remained in Britain. They threatened that without compliance, they would lock their hostages inside the

September has gained symbolic importance in the minds of Palestinian extremists and sympathetic Arab and Muslim groups.

airplanes and destroy them in the same fashion as the PanAm flight. After a few days, when negotiations stalled, the PFLP hijacked a fifth passenger jet, a BOAC VC-10 traveling from Bombay, India to Beirut, Lebanon, and forced it to join the two captured planes at Zarqa.

On September 12, the hijackers released some of the hostages, removed everyone from the three airplanes and destroyed them with dynamite in a series of dramatic explosions. Meanwhile, Jordan was trying to extricate itself from an embarrassing international situation. It treated the situation as a serious crime, but was accused by the Palestinian Liberation Organization (PLO) as being a 'traitor' to its Arab brethren. On September 17, fighting erupted between PLO and Jordanian forces, and Syria threatened to intervene on behalf of the PLO against Jordan. In an unprecedented move, Jordan appealed for assistance not only from Britain and the U.S., but also from Israel. Two weeks later, Britain, Switzerland and West Germany capitulated to the PFLP demands, releasing Khaled and six convicted Fedayeen terrorists in exchange for the remaining hostages. Jordan successfully drove the PLO forces from its territory without assistance, although the PFLP hijackers escaped with those fleeing forces.

This episode became known in fundamentalist Islamic groups as 'Black September,' as it represented a growing split between moderate and extreme groups in the Arab world; for extremists, the prospect of inter-Arab fighting emphasized the need to adhere to radical principles in order to defeat the more moderate elements of Arab culture who were viewed as surrendering to certain 'evils' such as the existence of the state of Israel.

Consequently, the month of September gained symbolic importance in the minds of Palestinian extremists and sympathetic Arab and Muslim groups. The Black September terrorist organization grew out of this memorialized concept, and on September 5, 1972, it executed the Munich Olympic Massacre of eleven Israeli atheletes. It also directed terrorist acts against Arab governments whose views were criticized by extremists as too moderate. On September 5, 1973, Palestinian terrorists seized the Saudi Arabian embassy in Paris, taking five hostages, and on September 26, 1976, Abu Nidal terrorists took ninety hostages at the Semiramis Hotel in Damascus, Syria.

Later events repeatedly ignited Palestinian rage, and only reinforced the sense that September was a sacred month of revolution. In September, 1978, the Camp David accords, which reconciled Israel and Egypt, were finalized, and on September 15, 1982, Israel invaded Beirut, Lebanon. On that same day, Black September terrorists seized the Egyptian embassy in Madrid, demanding that Egypt withdraw from its agreements with Israel. On September 23, 1983, an Omani Gulf Airbus traveling from Karachi, Pakistan to Abu Zabi, United Arab Emirates was brought down by a bomb, killing 111 people.

On September 20, 1984, Islamic Jihad killed fourteen and injured seventy with a suicide car bombing of the U.S. embassy in Lebanon. These types of activities continued on and off until the Israeli-PLO peace agreement was signed in Washington, D.C. on September 13, 1993, which marked a temporary lull in regional tensions.

A number of important conclusions can be drawn from the Black September episode and subsequent events. First, those who claim that the events of September 11, 2001 heralded a 'new' type of terrorism are misguided; although it was the first time a series of hijackings were combined with suicide missions to yield disastrous results, audacious, simultaneous hijackings and detonations of multiple commercial airliners were taking place over thirty years before. Second, the idea that most or all Palestinians, Muslims, Arabs or Arab governments are vehemently opposed to the U.S., Europe, and Israel is wrong. Divisions within and among Arab states, for example, over

foreign policies regarding the U.S. and Israel are ongoing, and extremist elements in those states are oftentimes as opposed to more moderate elements within their own societies as they are to a state such as Israel. Third, the historical context suggests an explanation for the timing of the World Trade Center and Pentagon attacks. The attacks were planned well in advance of their execution; if there were a time of symbolic importance when the attacks could be carried out, they likely would be planned in such a way as to coincide. Either the attacks were planned and carried out by individuals with Palestinian sympathies and/or extreme Pan-Arab or Islamic beliefs in line with the beliefs of groups such as al-Qaeda, Islamic Jihad, Abu Nidal, and Black September, or the events of September 11, 2001 represented a bizarre coincidence of timing.

TERRORISM

VIEWPOINTS AND DEFINITIONS

Political terrorism is psychological warfare waged through the media.
--Dr. Jerrold Post

Terrorism, traditionally, is violence aimed at the people who are watching. It is a kind of violent fear. Terrorists would kill a few to attract an audience of many.
--Brian Jenkins

Terrorism has been defined as the substate application of violence or threatened violence intended to sow panic in a society, to weaken or even overthrow the incumbents, and to bring about political change. It shades on occasion into guerrilla warfare (although unlike guerrillas, terrorists are unable or unwilling to take or hold territory) and even a substitute for war between states.
--Walter Laqueur

Terrorism is the premeditated, deliberate, systematic murder, mayhem, and threatening of the innocent to create fear and intimidation in order to gain a political or tactical advantage, usually to influence an audience.
--James M. Poland

Terrorism is the unlawful use or threat of violence against persons or property to further political or social objectives. It is usually intended to intimidate or coerce a government, individuals or groups, or to modify their behavior or politics.
--Vice-President's Task Force, 1986

Terrorism is the unlawful use of force or violence against persons or property to intimidate or coerce a government, the civilian population, or any segment thereof, in furtherance of political or social objectives.
--FBI

INTERNATIONAL TERRORISM - Activities that involve violent acts or acts dangerous to human life that are a violation of the criminal laws of the U.S. or of any State, or that would be a criminal violation if committed within the jurisdiction of the U.S. or of any State; appear to be intended to intimidate or coerce a civilian population; to influence the policy of a government by intimidation or coercion; or to affect the conduct of a government by assassination or kidnapping; and occur primarily outside the territorial jurisdiction of the U.S., or transcend national boundaries in terms of the means by which they are accomplished, the persons they appear intended to intimidate or coerce, or the locale in which their perpetrators operate or seek asylum.
--18 U.S.C.

Terrorism is an act carried out to achieve an inhuman and corrupt (mufsid) objective, and involving threat to security of any kind, and violation of rights acknowledged by religion and mankind.
--Ayatullah Shaykh Muhammad Ali Taskhiri, Vol V No. 1 (Muharram 1408 AH/1987 CE)

Terrorism is [inevitably] political in aims and motives; violent-or, equally important, threatens violence; designed to have far-reaching psychological repercussions beyond the immediate victim of target; conducted by an organization with an identifiable chain of command or conspiratorial cell structure (whose members wear no uniform or identifying insignia); and perpetrated by a sub-national group or non-state entity.
--Bruce Hoffman

State terrorism is a political system whose rule of recognition permits and/or imposes a clandestine, unpredictable, and diffuse application, even regarding clearly innocent people, of coercive means prohibited by the proclaimed judicial ordinance. State terrorism obstructs or annuls judicial activity and transforms the government into an active agent in the struggle for power.
--Ernesto Garzón

Narco-terrorism is conducted to further the aims of drug traffickers. It may include assassinations, extortion, hijackings, bombings, and kidnappings directed against judges, prosecutors, elected officials, or law enforcement agents, and general disruption of a legitimate government to divert attention from drug operations.

--Department of Defense

WHAT IS TERRORISM?

The notorious difficulty of defining 'terrorism' is a problem which has plagued academics, lawyers and practitioners of public policy for decades. The most common incarnation of this controversy comes in the form of the familiar aphorism, 'one man's terrorist is another man's freedom fighter.' This idea of subjectivity raises the crucial question of whether or not it is possible to come up with a clear and useful definition of terrorism which is *politically neutral*. In other words, are there actions which should be considered criminal regardless of the nobility of the cause championed by the perpetrator? This question is extremely important for justifying criminal prosecutions, military operations, and intrusive intelligence-gathering in cases where would-be terrorists offer excuses for their actions based on their political motivations, or where states such as Afghanistan and Sudan shelter such individuals from extradition or prosecution for political reasons.

This section looks at the problem of defining terrorism by considering three important issues: why terrorism is so difficult to define, how the international community has addressed these challenges, and what elements of agreement are shared among the vast majority of states in the world. The goal of this section is to disentangle the murky and politically-charged dialogue on the subject in order to clarify what

actions are under discussion and where international agreement lies.

WHY IS TERRORISM SO DIFFICULT TO DEFINE?

There are at least four reasons why the definition of terrorism has been controversial in domestic and international politics. First, in the history of terrorism, understandings of the term have changed significantly. Second, in modern times, the use of the term by states and the media has been inconsistent and confusing. Third, even within a single state like the U.S., multiple definitions exist across different government agencies with different responsibilities. Fourth, there is international political disagreement over the use of the term.

HISTORICAL EVOLUTION OF THE TERM

The popular meaning of the word 'terrorism' has changed significantly since its inception: during the French Revolution, it actually had a positive connotation! Terrorism contributed to the consolidation of the new government's power by intimidating counter-revolutionaries, and was a term associated with democracy. In the nineteenth century, anarchists proudly adopted the label 'terrorist' to refer to themselves and their prime weapon of assassination, as did anti-tsarist movements in Russia. It was not until the twentieth century that terrorism was used to describe specific criminal action. The 1930s saw a number of international conferences which were aimed at the prevention and punishment of

terrorism, which was conceived of as a crime against a state with the intention of causing terror in the minds of people, groups of people, or the general public. Nevertheless, these efforts were stymied by the onset of world war. During and immediately after World War II, uses of the word 'terrorism' shifted from the concept of an individual crime back to an instrument of government policy. Contrasted with the French Revolution, terrorism in this case was not considered noble, instead referring to policies of Adolf Hitler and Joseph Stalin. Since then, the substate revolutionary aspect of terrorism has returned to the common vernacular, leading to our current, rather confused situation, where a number of historical conceptions of terrorism are used simultaneously.

At the risk of oversimplifying, the one major characteristic of terrorism that *has* changed completely since its first use is that it is now considered morally reprehensible. It is not a label to claim with pride, it is a stigma to avoid at all costs. The last terrorist organization to describe itself publicly as such was the Israeli group known as the Stern Gang, in the 1940s. Now, all apparently terrorist organizations use names that liken themselves to armies or instruments of liberation or defense, or that use neutral terms like 'The Base'; referring to one's own actions as 'terrorist' would be to brand them as criminal and illegitimate.

USE AND MISUSE OF THE TERM BY STATES AND THE MEDIA

Although everyone agrees today that terrorism is evil, people still don't agree on what exactly it is. Different opinions in the media and among politicians would range from computer hacking ('cyber-terrorism') to tree-spiking ('eco-terrorism'), and could even extend to the enforcement of anti-terrorist provisions! One need look no further than Libyan leader Muammar Qaddafi's description of the criminal conviction in the Hague of one of the accused bombers of Pan Am Flight 103 over Lockerbie, Scotland as a 'terrorist hostage-taking' initiated by the U.S. and Britain.

The popular media often contributes to the confusion by failing to distinguish the characteristics of these different conceptions of terrorism. Moreover, news reports sometimes improperly use words and phrases with different meanings interchangeably, such as 'terrorism' and 'guerilla warfare.' As the next section on how the international community has addressed the challenges of defining terrorism will indicate, there are specific features of terrorism which distinguish it from concepts such as guerilla warfare, and which are common among more narrow understandings of terrorism such as 'eco-terrorism' and 'state-terrorism.'

MULTIPLE DEFINITIONS FOR MULTIPLE PURPOSES

Another source of confusion regarding the definition of terrorism exists in differing definitions used by different agencies, even within the same government. A good example of this can be found in the U.S. Government. The U.S. State Department employs a broad conception of terrorism in order to allow a significant degree of flexibility for U.S. foreign policy in designating certain states as supporting terrorism and initiating intelligence-gathering projects. But in order to prosecute someone in a court of law or extradite someone on a criminal charge from a foreign country, however, more specificity is required. For this purpose, the U.S. uses a different, more narrow definition. The definition of terrorism is necessarily different according to the function of a particular element of a government branch or agency. As a consequence, any attempt at defining terrorism must be explicit about its intended use.

INTERNATIONAL POLITICAL DISAGREEMENT

The same reasons which led to an increase in terrorism during the post-war era also made it politically difficult to define. The so-called 'third wave' of decolonization, which began in the 1950s and 1960s, and which resulted in the birth of many new states which had formerly been colonies of states like Britain, France and Belgium, encouraged fights for national independence. Advances in communications technology also meant media coverage of compelling events could capture the world's attention immediately. As a result, disenfranchised and underfinanced groups with national independence in mind found terrorist acts to be a particularly effective way of gaining publicity for their causes and sympathy from developing countries who recently had overcome oppressive colonial regimes themselves. Moreover, Cold War superpower struggles for influence in developing countries also led to superpower-supported acts of terrorism intended to destabilize emerging regimes affiliated with the opponent. Although terrorism increased during this time, attempts to outlaw terrorism ran into problems because developing states claimed they never would have become independent without terrorism. They wanted an exception to any international law which outlawed terrorism in order to protect people who wanted to fight for their own freedom. These discussions focused on the need to distinguish unjustified terrorism from justified political resistance. Disagreements on this subject in the 1970s led to the failure of proposals to outlaw terrorism entirely.

When Cold War tensions began to decline in the mid- to late-1980s, and the wave of decolonization grew more distant from the status quo, more substantive agreement on the subject of terrorism became possible. As the following section indicates, there is substantial agreement on how to conceptualize terrorism in international law today.

HOW HAS THE INTERNATIONAL COMMUNITY ADDRESSED THESE CHALLENGES?

When instances of terrorism went on the rise in the 1960s and the world encountered political problems trying to draft a comprehensive anti-terrorism treaty, states had to find alternative solutions. Instead of addressing the problem all at once, they opted for a bit-by-bit approach which would establish certain specific actions as international crimes. The first example of this approach was the 1970 Hague Convention for the Suppression of Unlawful Seizure of Aircraft. This treaty turned aircraft hijacking into an international crime, and forced countries either to extra dite or prosecute hijacking suspects found in their territory without exception. This approach was successful because it did not take account of the motivations of hijackers: no matter which side you were on, the simple fact of performing a hijacking made it terrorism. Even if you were fighting for your country's freedom, hijacking was still a crime because it involved innocent people.

Since then, this model has been copied with different actions, and the list of actions falling under the umbrella designation of 'terrorism' has grown to include hijacking aircraft, sabotaging or bombing aircraft, attacks on airports, attacks on diplomats or other internationally protected people, hostage-taking, improper use of nuclear materials, hijacking boats, and terrorist bombing (including biological and chemical attacks).

Yet this list has gaps. A machine-gun attack on a marketplace, for example, does not seem to be covered by these international treaties, which means it could be more difficult to compel a country to extradite someone who has committed such an act and fled to a different country.

More recently, the idea of a general definition which failed because of disagreements in the 1970s has been brought back with the intention of covering these gaps. Used side-by-side, a list-based definition and a general definition of terrorism would create a more effective anti-terrorism regime, and would indicate the important areas of agreement on this subject around the world.

WHAT ELEMENTS OF AGREEMENT ARE SHARED AMONG THE VAST MAJORITY OF STATES IN THE WORLD?

The most common underlying feature of anti-terrorism treaties is the prohibition on targeting innocent civilians. The international community appears to detest the idea not only of victimizing innocents themselves, but using attacks on innocent people as a way of influencing or intimidating a third party like a government or a general civilian population. This fact is borne out by closer investigation of the primary sources associated with the drafting of each of these treaties. This idea is also common to the idea of war crimes.

If one looks at all of the definitions of terrorism that exist in the laws of countries around the world, certain common features jump out as well. Adding these common features together, a definition of terrorism that represents where most countries agree would be: terrorism constitutes hijacking aircraft, sabotaging or bombing aircraft, attacks on airports, attacks on diplomats or other internationally protected people, hostage-taking, improper use of nuclear materials, hijacking boats, terrorist bombing, or any other act which is intended to kill or seriously injure any individual who is not a member of the armed forces of a State in the course of military hostilities, with the intent to intimidate or coerce a civilian population, government, or international organization. This definition helps to distinguish terrorism from guerilla warfare by reference to their targets: if a group is resisting a government by engaging its military apparatus, it is more consistent with guerilla warfare; if that same group is attacking civilians instead, it is committing

acts of terrorism.

The definition also encompasses not only political, religious, and criminal goals, but also certain terrorist goals that seek to destabilize a society or a way of life. It is an accurate representation of the current prevailing conception of terrorism in international criminal law. This is validated by the conclusion in 1999 of a United Nations convention aimed at putting a financial squeeze on international terrorists. The International Convention for the Suppression of the Financing of Terrorism necessarily had to define terrorism in order to say which actions could not be supported by private donations. It ended up with a definition that listed the same actions included in our definition, and added a general definition which was 'Any other act intended to cause death or serious bodily injury to a civilian, or to any other person not taking an active part in the hostilities in a situation of armed conflict, when the purpose of such act, by its nature or context, is to intimidate a population, or to compel a government or an international organization to do or to abstain from doing any act.'

TYPES OF TERRORISM

Most definitions of terrorism assume it to have political implications, but when 'political' is eliminated from our consideration, it is easy to conceive of instances where local residents are terrorized into not talking about drug dealers in their neighborhood, as a form of criminal terrorism. Pathological terrorism, such as the amoral villain in many horror movies, and the stalking ex-spouse in domestic situations, is another form of terrorism that becomes evident when political considerations are not present. Terrorism is an effort to achieve results in cases of political and criminal terrorism; in pathological terrorism, the terrorism becomes an end in itself. That is not to say that some of the terrorists employed by political or criminal organizations are not independently pathological terrorists. Indeed, given the constraints of modern society, the best suited planners of terrorist acts are pathological terrorists.

Nation states have resorted to terrorism to control their own, conquered populations. The historical dispersion of the Jews by Assyria in the 7th century BC was an example of a deliberate policy of terror intended to subjugate a population. State terrorism is also reflected in the actions of the German State Secret Police (Gestapo), endowed with nearly unlimited powers of arrest and detention; backed up by courts which actively supported their work, the

Gestapo routinely used terror to achieve state goals.

Still under the umbrella of State Terrorism is State-Supported terrorism, usually externally directed. States have international goals which they may elect to pursue with extreme and violent means while avoiding the constraints of war. Terrorism, not officially sanctioned by the state, may still exist to support the goals of that state. Several Middle Eastern states have supported terrorists whose

The German army in World War II found that its soldiers became ineffective after they were ordered to execute 75 civilians with rifle shots.

target is Israel. These states cannot engage in declared war (or even official attacks) for fear of reprisals or international condemnation but instead support terrorist attacks while denying responsibility for them.

The most common category of terrorism is sub-state, or non-state terrorism. Its perpetrators are not members of an organized or recognized state. The nation in which they live, and the nation in which they hold citizenship has no knowledge of and subsequently is not responsible for their actions. This form of terrorism has five subtypes:

SINGLE ISSUE TERRORISM

Some terrorists and terrorist groups

tend to focus on one or several related issues such as gun control, abortion, or deforestation. This breed of terrorist employs traditional terrorist tactics such as bombs and explosives in an attempt to achieve a political agenda. Single Issue Terrorist attacks have traditionally been small scale attacks but certainly, as in the case of the Atlanta Abortion Clinic bombing, not any less capable of evoking terror.

EXTREMIST POLITICAL TERRORISM

Although some have divided this category into Right Wing Terrorism and Revolutionary or Left Wing Terrorism, both categories exhibit striking similarities. Those with beliefs at the extreme edges of the political spectrum are, by definition, marginalized in their political power. Their constituency is small; their political power is similarly small. Without a radical change in the political climate, their chance of increasing their power remains correspondingly limited. Terrorism, for them, becomes a means of driving some of the population from participating in governmental elections and other political activities. Typical terrorist related fear tactics are used to intimidate citizens affiliated with mainstream political parties. Governmental attempts to suppress these intimidation tactics may be viewed by politically neutral citizens as an attempt to limit the scope of their political options and may drive once politically ambiguous citizens into the arms of the extremists.

SEPARATIST TERRORISM

The ambition to establish a separate state can be independent of extreme political views. While left wing or right wing ideology may be a component of the dogma of separatists, the overwhelming drive is for the creation of an independent state. Terrorism may be directed internally within the region: at the government, or it may be directed at allies of the government with a goal of creating diplomatic pressure in support of the separatist state. Additional terrorist acts may target the commercial sector in an attempt to exact economic pressure. Separatist terrorism cannot operate successfully in a vacuum: the common strategy is to create a legitimate political organization which pursues separatist goals, and a parallel terrorist organization which can be disavowed.

RELIGIOUS TERRORISM

The two fringes of religion, that is, the conservative fundamentalist and the more radical contemporary spiritual groups, are each capable of embracing terrorism as a means to an end. Though many contemporary religious faiths are perfectly docile and the majority of fundamentalist conservatives are equally peaceful, there still exists the possibility for terrorist activity. Single issue terrorism and religious terrorism often coexist: Abortion rights extremists have used their faith to justify unspeakable acts of terror. It is in this rationalization, by means of religious doctrine, that we find the defining constraint of religious terrorism. Text, principle, or the words of a charismatic spiritual leader, that enable followers to pursue what they perceive to be religious purity through terroristic means is

what sets Religious Terrorism apart from other forms of terroristic activity. Though the bible and many other religious texts include passages that, when isolated, may supply potential terrorists with both direction and motivation, the majority of religious followers are capable of exposure to such passages without resorting to violent, anti-social behavior.

PATHOLOGICAL TERRORISM

Terrorism must be executed by individuals: The planners, the trainers, the actual bombers and killers. The German army in World War II found that its soldiers became ineffective after they were ordered to execute 75 civilians with rifle shots; the Holocaust required the establishment of concentration camps and a bureaucratic structure to depersonalize the effort to kill non-combatant human beings for the very reason that most of the soldiers in its army did not have the requisite pathological, disturbed emotional condition that would allow them to engage in the required killing. The Holocaust leaders, those who did direct and participate in gross human rights abuses were unarguably possessing of some degree of this pathological anti-social condition, however enhanced by culture, background, education, training, or conditioning.

To fly a passenger airplane into a world icon such as the World Trade Center, killing as many as 6000 civilians, unquestionably mandates a pilot-hijacker with a dysfunctional emotional composition. Certainly political and religious factors provided these men with what they perceived to be pragmatic rationalizations for their actions, but it was a pathological terrorism that lead this devastating mission to its deadly conclusion.

IS BIN LADEN A SOCIOPATH?

The APA list of symptoms for an anti-social personality disorder (popularly known as a sociopath) includes:

(1) failure to conform to social norms with respect to lawful behaviors as indicated by repeatedly performing acts that are grounds for arrest; (2) deceitfulness, as indicated by repeated lying, use of aliases, or conning others for personal profit or pleasure; (3) irritability and aggressiveness, as indicated by repeated physical fights or assaults; (4) reckless disregard for safety of self or others; (5) lack of remorse, as indicated by being indifferent to or rationalizing having hurt, mistreated, or stolen from another.

Captivating storytellers that exude self-confidence, they can spin a web that intrigues others. Since they are persuasive, they have the capacity to destroy their critics verbally or emotionally. They never recognize the rights of others and see their self-serving behaviors as permissible. They appear to be charming, yet are covertly hostile and domineering, seeing their victim as merely an instrument to be used. He dominates and humiliates his victims. Feels entitled to certain things as "his right." Craves adulation and attendance. Must be the center of attention with his own fantasies as the "spokesman for God," "enlightened," "leader of humankind," etc. Creates an us-versus-them mentality."
--cult expert Janja Lalich

FIGHTING TERRORISM

COPS OR SOLDIERS?

Following the attacks of September 11, 2001, a number of public officials made statements regarding the need to 'bring to justice' the organizers of the catastrophe, as well as the need to treat the attacks as an 'act of war' and 'hunt down' those responsible. These statements raise an important question of how to address the problem of terrorism: should it be treated as fighting a war, or fighting crime? Should it take the form of the Persian Gulf War, or should it take the form of the 'war on drugs'? Should it be fought with soldiers, or with police officers?

To answer this question, the first issue is whether or not the terrorism being discussed is state-sponsored. This can include everything ranging from a state which is aware that terrorism is organized within its borders and does nothing about it to a state which uses its own agents to perpetrate terrorist acts around the globe. In cases of state-sponsored terrorism, there is a good case for fighting the war with soldiers, since this is what militaries, simply put, are supposed to be good at, and since that is the only way to get to the root of the problem. If a state is sponsoring terrorism, simply arresting individual perpetrators when they are caught outside the borders of that state will do nothing to stop the overall problem. There will always be more people to take the place of those who are captured. But if the funding and support dries up, terrorism will be greatly reduced, which means military force may be required to compel a state to forego terrorism as a political tool.

Furthermore, if one state is funding terrorists with the intent to assist their attacks against another country, it is the same as using its military to attack that country. In this sense, it is undeniably an act of war.

If the terrorism does not have any connection with the state, then it is appropriate to consider the scale of the terrorist organization

to determine which type of force should be used. If the terrorists are on the scale of a small army in one location, and control certain sections of territory, or are likely to engage in military-like maneuvers against officials attempting to apprehend them, military force is probably required. This could take the form of a Special Operations force which is specially trained to locate specific targets hidden away. Given the reasonable expectation that deadly force will be used by these groups to resist apprehension, it is likely that this type of mission would be treated as a military operation, such that forces would not be required to follow traditional police procedures.

But if the scale of the terrorist organization in a particular location is small, law enforcement officials must be used and the analogy to an actual war becomes more like the 'war on drugs' and less like a military war. This is because the idea of a state declaring 'war' on an individual goes against the foundations of a democratic society. If the U.S. decided to use military forces to assassinate a suspected terrorist in an apartment

in Brooklyn, it would be going down a dangerous path which could justify assassinating people accused of other crimes, while also encountering serious problems in the event mistakes are made. What if they pick the wrong apartment? Apologies can be made for a mistaken arrest, but not for a mistaken assassination.

Of course, there are many complexities involved. If military force is deemed to be necessary, it has to be initiated in such a way as to avoid offending other nations, lest there be an overall increase in terrorism as a result. If law enforcement is required to apprehend a suspect in a different country, cooperation will be required so that authorities in that country can make the arrest. But the discussion above should make it clear that different approaches are warranted in different circumstances, and sometimes a combination of approaches will be required. As will become evident in the rest of this book, Osama bin Laden's Al Qaeda terrorist organization is the type of network which will probably require both approaches: military action in Afghanistan where he receives support from the government and has established military-style base camps with hundreds of soldiers, and cooperative law enforcement efforts around the globe to eliminate each cell in his loosely-organized network.

WHY US?

WHY THE U.S. IS A TARGET OF MIDDLE EASTERN-BASED TERRORIST ATTACKS

When looking for reasons why the U.S. is a target of international terrorist attacks, the explanations typically fall on U.S. policy towards the Middle East. Although policies in regions such as Latin America sometimes attract anti-U.S. terror campaigns, those policies do not arouse the same level of fervor, and the attacks often contain important domestic elements in the Latin American countries where they take place. The three features of U.S. policy in the Middle East which attract disfavor in Arab and Islamic communities consist of U.S. policy towards Israel, U.S. presence in Saudi Arabia and U.S. policy towards Iraq. To understand the rationale behind each of these policy areas, as well as why they cause anger, we must consider them in the context of the region's history.

Many Arabs believe that Israel is an illegitimate state, and resent the fact that the U.S. is so closely allied with it. The establishment of Israel as a state in 1948 came after over fifty years of efforts of Zionist leaders to establish a Jewish homeland in the form of a sovereign state. Britain administered the so-called 'Palestinian Territory,' and was responsible for the initial moves which permitted Jewish settlement of the area after 1917. Immigration increased during the 1920s and 1930s, and with it came increased tensions due to Palestinians' perception that Jews were taking their land

away from them. When it became clear that there was no end to the level of Nazi persecution of Jews in Germany, so many Jews attempted to flee to Palestine that Britain began to turn them away and send them back to Germany in order to keep the situation in Palestine stable. After World War II, it became clear that this was a horrible mistake, and there can be no doubt that the Holocaust and subsequent guilt was a major factor in the creation of the State of

---

Many Arabs believe that Israel is an illegitimate state, and resent the fact that the U.S. is so closely allied with it.

Israel under the auspices of the newly-founded United Nations. The UN decided to split the Palestinian Territory into two sections: one Jewish state, the other, an Arab state. Jerusalem was to be in the middle, administered as an international city by the UN.

Violence immediately erupted between Arabs and Jews, and on May 14, 1948, Jewish leaders unilaterally proclaimed the existence of Israel. The next day, neighboring Arab states launched a military invasion, and war continued until 1949. Eventually a peace agreement was reached, with Israeli borders declared. But border violence continued, and in October 1956, Israel invaded and occupied the Gaza Strip and Egypt's Sinai

Peninsula at the same time French and British forces were fighting against Egyptian forces over rights to control the Suez Canal. Israeli forces withdrew five months later, replaced by a UN force, but tensions flared again in May, 1967 when Egyptian President Gamal Abdel Nasser expelled the UN troops and replaced them with heavily-fortified Egyptian forces on the Israeli border. Israel then mounted a blistering pre-emptive attack against Egypt, Jordan and Syria, and in what came to be known as the 'Six Day War,' Israel took possession of Egypt's Sinai Peninsula, the Gaza Strip, Syria's Golan Heights and Jordan's West Bank of the Jordan River, including East Jerusalem.

On October 6, 1973, Syrian and Egyptian forces launched a surprise attack against Israel on Yom Kippur, the Jewish Day of Atonement, in hopes of regaining the territory lost in 1967. Israel lost ground at first, but ended up pushing Syrian and Egyptian forces back farther than where they started from, even taking control of the Suez canal. The U.S. and U.S.S.R. mediated a cease-fire agreement, and five months later, Israel withdrew its forces from the Suez Canal.

Eventually, the relationship between Egypt and Israel warmed, and in 1977, Egyptian President Anwar Sadat visited Jerusalem at the invitation of Israeli Prime Minister Menachem Begin. Sadat recognized Israel's right to exist, and established the basis for further negotiations. In September 1978, Sadat and Begin met with U.S. President Jimmy Carter at Camp David, and in 1979, they signed the 'Camp David Accords' which provided for the return to Egypt of the Sinai Peninsula, principles for the transition of the West Bank and Gaza Strip to an autonomous territory, and peace between Egypt and Israel. Sadat was later murdered by extremist Arab terrorists for signing this agreement.

Although Israel was making peace on its southern border, it was making war on its northern border. Considering Palestinian guerilla forces residing in Lebanon to be a security threat, Israel invaded Lebanon in 1978. Israel withdrew at the request of the UN, but invaded again in 1982 to fight the newly-organized guerilla group, the Palestine Liberation Organization (PLO). Israel kept its forces in Lebanon until the year 2000 in order to maintain a 'security zone' between the two countries.

After the Gulf War, opportunities emerged for peace in the Middle East, and on September 13, 1993, Israel and the PLO signed an agreement at the White House in Washington, D.C. which established a substantive plan for transferring power in Palestine from Israel to the newly-created Palestinian Authority. On September 28, 1995, Israeli Prime Minister Yitzhak Rabin and Palestinian Authority President Yasser Arafat signed the Interim Agreement which went further in establishing the organizational structure necessary for Palestine to become a state. Just one month later, an extremist Jewish terrorist assassinated Rabin for signing that agreement.

Progress continued in October 1998, when Israeli Prime Minister Benjamin Netanyahu and President Arafat signed the Wye River Accords in Maryland which gave more power to Palestinian security forces. Nevertheless, conflict erupted again in September 2000 following a controversial visit to Haram-al-Sharif/ The Temple Mount by right-wing Israeli politician Ariel Sharon, who was elected Israeli Prime Minister. This area is one of Islam's most sacred sites, and the location of an important mosque, while it is the holiest site for Jews, as it is the location of an ancient temple destroyed by the Romans.

From this history, it is possible to see how a version of events could develop which views the existence of Israel as built on 'stolen' land, and that subsequent conflicts and occupations by Israel represent a continuation of this land-grabbing. This version of events would require not negotiation with Israel, but its destruction due to its illegitimacy, and this is precisely the opinion of radical Arab and Islamic extremists. This also explains why they would attack their own governments for negotiating and reaching peace with Israel.

Given this potential interpretation, it is also possible to see how the resulting anger could be assigned to states allied with Israel. The U.S. is viewed as the major facilitator of Israel's military attacks on its Arab neighbors, since it offers Israel hundreds of millions of dollars worth of military aid and high technology weaponry. Were it not for the U.S., Israel would not have nearly the military capabilities it does, and its policy potentially would have been less aggressive; at the same time, this could have made the prospect of a successful Arab invasion greater. At any rate, U.S. commitment towards Israel is partially due to its post-World War II history, and largely a result of the 'Jewish Lobby.' With a large and influential Jewish population in the U.S., American foreign policy towards Israel has historically had very little room for flexibility. As a result, the U.S. is often viewed with exactly the same contempt held for Israel in extreme Arab and Islamic circles.

But in terms of its physical presence, the U.S. has played more of a role in the Persian Gulf. This is due mainly to U.S. interest in oil. Saudi Arabia produces more oil than any other country in the world (it has 25% of the world's total oil), and the U.S. depends on it for supply. Consequently, U.S. policy in the Persian Gulf is concentrated mostly on protecting Saudi Arabia.

This was literally how the U.S. and Saudi Arabia forged their first relations. In 1945, U.S. President Franklin D. Roosevelt and Saudi King Abdel-Aziz ibn Saud established an agreement that the U.S. would always protect the Saudi royal family against all opponents in return for ongoing U.S. access to Saudi oil. This has played out not only in terms of U.S. protection of Saudi Arabia against external enemies, but also against internal enemies.

Operation Desert Shield was implemented as the first phase of U.S. plans to deal with the Iraqi invasion of Kuwait in 1990 as a way to protect Saudi oil fields from a possible Iraqi invasion. Although Operation Desert Storm was aimed at liberating Kuwait, the U.S. interest in protecting Saudi oil was always an important driving concern in the region. Since then, the U.S. has maintained a strong military presence in Saudi Arabia, and used airfields there to patrol and enforce no-fly zones over Iraq. But the U.S. has also armed and trained the Saudi Arabian National Guard, the instrument of an oppressive domestic regime which maintains order at the expense of real civil rights. Maintaining order is important to the U.S., which would not like to see an overthrow of the Saudi regime by Islamic radicals as was the case in 1979 in Iran.

From this, it is possible to see the version of events which results in anger against the U.S. First, the Saudi regime is perceived by more fundamentalist Muslims as a 'sellout,' and the U.S. is seen as the tempting force which, with its money, has compelled the Saudis to permit the U.S. military to use its bases and exert influence over the region. Second, the simple fact of a U.S. presence in Saudi Arabia is viewed by some Muslims as trampling on sacred territory. Since Saudi Arabia is the birthplace of Muhammed, and consequently, of the Islamic faith, a U.S. military presence is especially desecrating. Saudi Arabian rules say that non-Muslims may not even enter the country, unless it is for business. An even more restrictive version of this rule dates back to just after the Crusades in the Middle Ages. Thus, Muslims around the world may feel this presence to be a personal affront.

But if Saudi Arabia is perceived to be a corrupt regime, Kuwait certainly falls into a similar category for some Muslims. And if Kuwait is corrupt, then the Iraqi invasion of Kuwait in 1990 may not be perceived as wrong - in fact, it could be perceived as 'saving' it from harmful Western influences. If this is true, then it would be the U.S., whose military operations at the beginning of the 1990s repelled the Iraqi invasion, who would be wrong. This kind of tortured logic may seem outrageous to Western observers who believe in the inherent justice of saving a sovereign country from being invaded, but to some members of extremist Islamic groups, it is an additional reason to despise the U.S. As a result, the so-called 'facts' of history can be perceived in radically different ways, and can be the sources of significant grievances.

TERRORIST GROUPS

WHERE ARE THEY LOCATED

17 November
Greece

Abu Sayyaf Group
Philippines

**Al-Gama'a al-Islamiyya
The Islamic Group)**
Egypt

Al Qaeda (The Base)
Afghanistan

**Armed Islamic Group
(GIA)**
Algeria

Aum Shiryinko
Japan

**Democractic Front
for the Liberation of
Palestine**
Palestine

**Euskadi ta Askatasuna
(ETA, Basque Fatherland
and Liberty)**
Spain

**Fatah Revolutionary
Council(Abu Nidal, Black
September)**
Lebanon

Hamas
Palestine

Harakat ul-Ansar (HUA)
Pakistan

Hezb'allah (Party of God)
Lebanon

**Islamic Movement of
Uzbekistan**
Uzbekistan

Jamaat ul-Fuqra
Pakistan

Japanese Red Army
Japan

**Jihad Group (Islamic
Jihad)**
Egypt

Kach and Kahane Chai
Israel

**Kosovo Liberation Army
(KLA)**
Kosovo

**Kurdish Worker's Party
(PKK)**
Turkey

Ku Klux Klan (KKK)
United States

Lautaro Youth Movement
Chile

**Loyalist Volunteer Force
(LVF)**
Northern Ireland

**Moranzanist Patriotic
Front**
Honduras

Mujihadeen-e Khalq
Iran

**National Liberation Army
(ELN)**
Columbia

New People's Army
Philippines

**Palestine Liberation
Front (PLF)**
Iraq

Palestinian Islamic Jihad
Palestine

**Party of Democratic
Kampuchea (Khmer Rouge)**
Cambodia

**Popular Front for the
Liberation of Palestine
(PFLP)**
Palestine

Popular Struggle Front
Syria

Quibla
South Africa

Real IRA
Northern Ireland

Red Army Faction
Germany

Red Brigades
Italy

**Revolutionary Armed
Forces of Colombia
(FARC)**
Colombia

**Revolutionary People's
Struggle**
Greece

**Sendero Luminoso
(Shining Path)**
Peru

Tupac Amaru
Peru

This list is not comprehensive, but includes some of the more significant terrorist operations currently operating around the world.

Most of these organizations do not specifically target Americans, directing their violence locally towards their own governments or specific sections of their own country's population based on religion or ethnicity. The majority have as their goal national self-determination or the overthrow of their country's present government. A few, such as Aum Shiryinko in Japan, are more cult-like. This group orchestrated the world's first chemical weapons terrorist attack when it released deadly Sarin nerve gas in the Tokyo subway.

By no means do all of these groups operate with the blessings of their own governments. The vast majority do not, as their targets are actually their own governments. However, organizations that direct their violence internationally such as Al Qaeda and Hezb'allah are more likely to receive support from their own countries' governments and from the governments of allied countries. Governments which are generally acknowledged to support terrorism are Afghanistan, Iran, Iraq, Lebanon, Sudan and Syria.

WHO IS OSAMA BIN LADEN?

Osama bin Laden, an exiled Saudi Arabian multi-millionaire, is perhaps the world's most prominent, yet mysterious, terrorist. What is his background, and what are his motivations? What are his grievances against the U.S, and why does he organize attacks against us?

Osama bin Laden was born in 1951 in Riyadh, the political capital of Saudi Arabia. He was the youngest of over 20 children born into a wealthy family with a prosperous construction business. Little is known of his childhood, although as a university student in the early 1970s, he had mentors who had been exiled from Egypt due to their extreme interpretations of Islam.

In 1979, the Soviet Union invaded Afghanistan in order to prop up the faltering Communist regime which held power. Many Arabs, including bin Laden, considered this a call to arms for all followers of the Muslim faith. Bin Laden traveled to Peshawar, Pakistan, on the Pakistani-Afghan border, and established an organization called 'al-Qaeda,' or, 'the Base.' The purpose of this organization was to funnel money, arms and supplies to the *mujihadeen* rebels who were fighting to overthrow the Afghan Communist regime and expel the Soviet forces from the country. This organization also recruited non-Afghan Muslims to join the fight, and successfully attracted thousands of volunteers as well as many private donations and public financial contributions.

When the Soviet Union withdrew from Afghanistan in defeat in 1989, bin Laden had gained cult leader-like prominence among the non-Afghan Muslim warriors (known locally as 'Arab Afghans') he had recruited, who now were stuck in central Asia with no more invaders to repel. He moved back to Saudi Arabia, and soon found a new cause: at the end of 1990, U.S. troops began arriving on Saudi soil in large numbers, preparing to launch a massive military operation against the Iraqi army in Operation Desert Storm.

Bin Laden was furious. He considered the Americans' arrival a desecration of Arabia, the historic and sacred homeland of the prophet Muhammad. He began organizing militant opposition to the ruling Saudi royal family, and was eventually kicked out of his own country for smuggling arms to opposition groups. He moved to Sudan, where he began to orchestrate terrorist attacks in the hope that they would lead to the U.S. withdrawing its ongoing military presence from Saudi Arabia. These attacks included the February 26, 1993 World Trade Center bombing, the November 13, 1995 car bomb in Riyadh, Saudi Arabia, and the June 25, 1996 bombing of the Khobar Towers complex in Dhahran, Saudi Arabia.

The United States put intense diplomatic pressure on Sudan to expel bin Laden from its territory, and was successful. But in a clear example of "Be careful what you wish for: you just might get it," when Sudan expelled bin Laden, he fled to Afghanistan, which was coming under control of the fundamentalist Taliban movement. This put him in a much more isolated, remote, and ultimately safer location. Only after his arrival in Afghanistan did the U.S. realize it had had enough evidence to request the extradition of bin Laden from Sudan for the 1993 World Trade Center bombing.

When bin Laden returned to Afghanistan, he found a hospitable political climate which matched his radical interpretations of Islam. He was accepted as a 'guest' of the Taliban, a concept based on ancient Bedouin and other tribal traditions, which dictates that guests may stay as long as they wish in order to facilitate life and transportation in a harsh and forbidding desert climate.

Osama bin Laden quickly gained the favor of Taliban leader Mullah Omar, simultaneously reuniting and drawing in the 'Arab Afghans' he had recruited in the 1980s. Until then, the Taliban did not interact with the Arab Afghans; afterwards, Omar began to issue venomous statements about the U.S., the U.N., and Saudi Arabia. This was language which had not been used by the Taliban before bin Laden arrived.

On February 23, 1998, bin Laden issued perhaps his most famous *fatwa*, or 'edict,' in a London-based Arabic newspaper. This was a declaration of *jihad*, or 'holy war,' against what he called 'the Jews and the Crusaders.' This declaration offers great insight into what motivates bin Laden and why he detests the U.S. enough to attack its civilians.

He listed three grievances: first, the presence of U.S. forces in Saudi Arabia, which desecrates the Islamic holyland and humiliates Muslims; second, the attacks and sanctions on Iraq, which have caused over one million deaths in that country; and third, the U.S. alliance with Israel, which is unjustly occupying and killing Muslims in Jerusalem. He claimed that these three crimes constituted a 'declaration of war by the Americans against God, his Prophet, and the Muslim people.'

If, as he says, the U.S. is declaring war in an offensive attack, thereby putting Islamic states on the defensive, Islamic law would seem to suggest that it is a personal duty of every Muslim to fight back. This explains his edict, which says, therefore, 'To kill Americans and their allies, both civilian and military, is an individual duty of every Muslim who is able, in any country where this is possible, until the Aqsa Mosque and the Haram Mosque are released from their grip and until their armed forces, decimated and broken-winged, depart from all the lands of Islam, unable to threaten any Muslim.' The Aqsa Mosque is located on the Temple Mount/Haram-al- Sharif in the middle of Jerusalem, and is the most hotly contested piece of land among Jews and Muslims in all of Israel, and the Haram Mosque is Islam's holiest site in Mecca. He goes on to say that it is Allah's command 'to kill the Americans and plunder their possessions,' referring to Americans as 'demons' and America's allies as 'helpers of Satan.'

A few months after issuing this particular *fatwa* on August 7, 1998,

suicide bombers driving cars laden with explosives simultaneously destroyed both the U.S. Embassy in Nairobi, Kenya, as well as the U.S. Embassy in Dar es Salaam, Tanzania, killing a total of 301 people and injuring well over 5,000. On October 12, 2000, suicide bombers on a small boat crippled the U.S.S. Cole in Yemen. Each of these attacks has been associated with bin Laden's organization. In particular, convincing evidence arose out of the New York federal trials of the surviving perpetrators of the embassy bombings.

After the embassy bombings,

the U.S. fired Tomahawk cruise missiles at what were believed to be terrorist training camps in Afghanistan, as well as what was believed to be a chemical weapons manufacturing plant in Sudan. As it turned out, the plant in Sudan was a bona fide pharmaceuticals plant. The status of the camps in Afghanistan was unclear, although reports indicated with credible evidence that two of the missiles struck a rural school and a mosque. It appears that the attack only bolstered the popularity of Osama bin Laden among extremist Muslims, reinforcing beliefs in his invincibility and attaching greater importance to him as the target of a superpower.

Although many assume bin Laden's anger to stem from U.S.-Israeli relations, this analysis suggests his motivations to be more complex, and to focus more on U.S. military presence in Saudi Arabia and policies towards Iraq. Today, Osama bin Laden most likely lives in the mountainous land near the Taliban's spiritual capital, Kandahar, although his precise whereabouts at a given moment are unknown due to his frequent changes of location. His locations were better known in previous years due to his trackable use of cellular and satellite phones. Now, he entrusts most communication to his associates, or conducts face-to-face meetings. His personal wealth, accumulated from family inheritance and government and private donations, is estimated at $270 million.

THE AL QAEDA ORGANIZATION

George W. Bush and the U.S. Government have declared war on terrorism, and in particular, on Osama bin Laden's Al Qaeda terrorist network. But to understand how this war could be executed and won, one must understand the nature of this organization. What is the history of Al Qaeda? How is it organized? How many people are involved, and where are they located? Will capturing Osama bin Laden disrupt the Al Qaeda organization?

Just like the concept of an innovative business model would dawn on a management consultant, so the realization of a terrorist network with global reach struck an enthusiastic Osama bin Laden in 1987. He was one of the leaders and head recruiters of a Pan-Islamic movement which drew Muslims from across the globe to fight on behalf of the mujihadeen rebels against the Soviet invasion and occupation of Afghanistan. This was organized in the form of a Pakistani agency known as the Office of Services.

This recruiting and training office began with just a few Arabs who included religious teachings in their program of recruitment. It began with difficulty by attempting to teach religious lessons to Afghan rebels; the Arabs spoke Arabic, but did not speak any of the Afghan languages. But over time, not only did a successful religious program evolve, which later merged with a militant Pakistani political party, but the movement successfully attracted thousands of Muslims, mostly from Arab states, to fight for the Afghan cause. The thought occurred to Osama bin Laden that if he could successfully extract thousands of would-be holy warriors from a worldwide Muslim population for a jihad in Afghanistan, he might be able to motivate the same individuals to participate in a jihad on a global level, targeting corrupted and moderate Islamic states and 'infidel' Western states such as the U.S.

Osama bin Laden entered into discussions with a radical Egyptian terrorist group known as Islamic Jihad, the group which assassinated Egyptian President Anwar Sadat in 1981 for signing a peace deal with Israel. One of the individuals involved in these early discussions was the cleric Sheik Omar Abdel Rahman, who eventually moved to New York to found an Office of Services branch there, and ended up being convicted in 1995 for planning to explode important buildings in New York City including the World Trade Center and the United Nations.

The result of the discussions in 1987 was to create a smaller branch of the Office of Services which would use separate training camps in Afghanistan and Pakistan to deal exclusively with recruiting and training Muslims for a global jihad. They decided to name this branch 'The Base,' or in Arabic, 'Al Qaeda.'

The influx of Muslims was continuing, and the movement was gathering force. When the Soviet Union withdrew from Afghanistan in 1989, some of these self-named 'Arab-Afghans' remained in Afghanistan and Pakistan attempting to spread their radical interpretations of Islam to others, while others returned to their homelands to foment rebellion there. The victory against a superpower instilled a headstrong confidence in many of the participants in that war which reinforced the belief that such a victory could be replicated across the world in a global jihad.

One example is Algeria, where Arab Afghans returned home and founded the Groupe Islamique Armi (GIA, Armed Islamic Group) in 1991. This group became one of the most brutal terrorist groups in Africa, massacring Algerian Muslims who were 'non-believers' in the concept of jihad, and contributing greatly to the murders of over 75,000 Algerians and 'disappearances' of 20,000 in the past eight years. Not only was this group founded by bin Laden associates, but it receives funding from him as well.

When bin Laden was exiled from his home country of Saudi Arabia, he moved to Sudan and continued to develop the Al Qaeda organization with camps in Sudan and Afghanistan, as well as the establishment of legitimate businesses to help fund the cause. He broadened the group to include extremist Muslims from around the world, and when U.S. troops entered Somalia in 1993, he created an Al Qaeda cell in Kenya which later participated in a massive gun battle with U.S. special forces, killing 18 Americans and hundreds of Somalis. This Kenyan branch planned and carried out the 1996 bombing of the U.S. Embassy in Nairobi, Kenya.

Around this same time, another member of Al Qaeda tried, but did not succeed in purchasing enriched uranium in Europe.

The U.S. only became aware of this movement in 1996 when it became clear that officials had mistranslated Arabic language evidence in the 1993 World Trade Center bombing trials.

One piece of evidence was a bomb manual seized from one of the suspects of that crime who had spent time in Pakistan. The manual was originally translated as being dated 1982, published in Amman, Jordan, and with page headings saying 'The Basic Rule.' In 1996, Federal investigators became aware of the mistake in translation: that the publication date was 1989 (two years after the founding of bin Laden's group), the place of publication was Afghanistan, and the heading on each page was not 'The Basic Rule,' but rather 'The Base.'

After bin Laden found safe haven in Afghanistan in 1996, he consolidated

his position there, and a mutually beneficial relationship began between Al Qaeda and the Taliban regime which was rising to power. Since then, his terrorist network has orchestrated a number of attacks against the United States, and is widely suspected of participating in the September 11, 2001 attacks on the World Trade Center and the Pentagon.

The Al Qaeda terrorist network operates in something resembling a franchise operation: it has franchises around the globe which receive

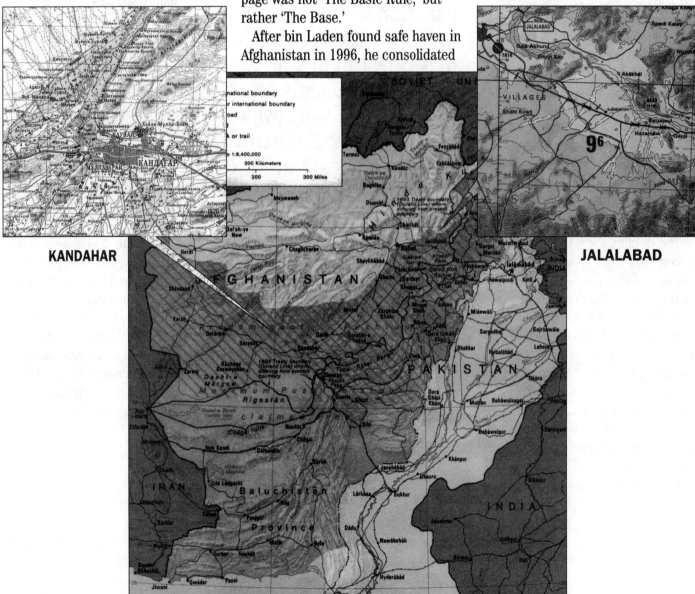

KANDAHAR

JALALABAD

instructions, guidance, and sometimes funding from a central source, but which operate independently of each other. This makes it an exceptionally difficult organization to eliminate. Capturing members of one cell in one city does not guarantee making inroads into the larger organization, since the members of one cell do not usually even know the members of cells in other locations.

Nevertheless, it is clear that the headquarters is in Afghanistan. Al Qaeda runs approximately twelve training camps there which have trained 5,000 terrorists over the past ten years. These terrorists have returned to their homes in over 50 different countries to establish cells and operate as 'sleeper agents' who blend into the society and lead otherwise normal lives before organizing terror strikes. These countries include both Islamic and non-Islamic states, from Malaysia to Great Britain, and from the Philippines to the United States.

The training these terrorist hopefuls receive involves an education in explosives manufacturing, small arms and logistics. Reports indicate that the 1998 U.S. Embassy bombings were rehearsed on replica models constructed at one of Al Qaeda's training camps in Afghanistan. One camp specializes in using commercially available products to develop chemical bombs, poisons and poison gases which are tested on dogs and rabbits tethered to outdoor posts on the camp's firing range.

Al Qaeda uses mobile and satellite phones, encrypted e-mail and CD-ROM data storage for communication, although these modes of communication are not used anymore by the highest leadership for fear of being traced and located by

> Although Al Qaeda has short term goals of forcing a U.S. withdrawal of military force from Saudi Arabia, an end to sanctions against Iraq, and the establishment of a Palestinian state, its long term goals are to promote a worldwide jihad which will destroy Western states and result in Islamic Law ruling the globe.

intelligence officials from the U.S. and elsewhere.

With the fatwa issued by Osama bin Laden in 1998, it became clear that the targets of Al Qaeda were not limited to military targets, but explicitly included women, children,

and any and all American civilians, in addition to civilians in other Islamic countries as well as Israel.

Osama bin Laden has already dictated a succession line in the event of his death or capture. This means it is already clear who will take over if bin Laden is killed, captured or handed over to prosecutors in the U.S. Consequently, any U.S. attempts to stamp out the Al Qaeda organization in Afghanistan will have to do a thorough job of locating individuals in the highest levels of the group.

Although Al Qaeda has short term goals of forcing a U.S. withdrawal of military force from Saudi Arabia, an end to sanctions against Iraq, and the establishment of a Palestinian state, its long term goals are to promote a worldwide jihad which will destroy Western states and result in Islamic Law ruling the globe. With a goal of this type, it appears that normal political discussions are not possible, and the final outcome is non-negotiable.

Finally, it should be mentioned that while Al Qaeda is the most prominent and well-organized terrorist network based in Afghanistan, it is not the only one. In addition to the 5,000 militants who have trained in Al Qaeda camps, over 50,000 more have trained in camps operated by separate groups and organizations about whom less is known.

PROFILES IN TERRORISM

The World Trade Center and Pentagon attacks raised an important question: what kind of person would commandeer a civilian airliner and fly it on a suicide mission into a building? Preventing terrorism of this kind in the future requires not only understanding the Osama bin Ladens of the world, but also requires understanding the people who work under him and carry out his orders or wishes, oftentimes to their own death.

Bin Laden's terrorist organization is set against a background of conditions which facilitate the recruitment of new volunteers. In many parts of the world, most notably North Africa, the Middle East and Central and South Asia, the economic backwardness of the regions exist in stark contrast to what is viewed as an opulent Western lifestyle. For many Muslims, political and religious grievances merge, including the strong U.S. military presence on Saudi Arabian soil, as well as what is viewed as U.S. mistreatment of Iraq through punishing sanctions that are starving the population. Coupled with U.S. support of Israel, which is viewed as a regional bully and even an illegitimate state, followers of Islam can point to a number of examples of injustice.

The people who consider these grievances to be enough to fight in a terrorist movement are typically on the extreme fringe of Islamic society. This makes Afghanistan the perfect starting point for joining such a cause; as it is by far the most strict and con-servative Muslim regime in the world, extremists view it as a romantic ideal, and a pure and uncompromising incarnation of the type of society they hope for a 'real' Islamic country, as one rebel put it. Since there is a battle raging against the Northern Alliance 'infidels,' the opportunity for true jihad presents itself, and the call is answered by those Muslims who believe it is their personal duty to join.

Osama bin Laden has ripe pickings of these individuals who come to Afghanistan out of a sense of personal duty. He trains them not only for terrorism, but also to fight for the Taliban against the Northern Alliance, and for Pakistan in Kashmir. He appeals to them due to his fanatical and unwavering commitment to his principles, and his ability to focus their grievances on specific targets such as the United States, Israel, and regional enemies of the Taliban including more moderate Islamic regimes. He offers easy answers to complex problems, and gives meaning to people's lives, going so far as to promise them a place in Heaven if they martyr themselves for the cause.

Individuals who join the Al Qaeda terrorist network are almost always young Muslim men who hold an Islamic ideal close to their hearts, along with a number of grievances. They come from around the world to be trained in Afghanistan to fight a holy war wherever they are needed. Psychologically, these are generally desperate young men who attain a sense of freedom, self-importance, power and group camaraderie from membership in bin Laden's loosely-knit organization. A 21-year old recruit once said: "When you have a gun, you feel invincible."

Most new recruits come from universities and religious seminaries across the Muslim world. Some far right-wing Islamic seminaries have been known to pay the travel expenses of students traveling to Afghanistan for 'schooling.' But by all accounts, recruits have come from over sixty different countries, including the United States and Great Britain.

The two most common characteristics are a need to belong to a group and a conviction that they represent the 'true believers.' They project their same antisocial motivations on their opposition, creating a threatening vision of the world as a state of nature, a 'kill or be killed' situation. This enables them to imagine their enemy as pure evil, thus dehumanizing them and creating a clarity of motivation without any moral ambiguity as to the rightness of the cause. Without pangs of conscience, the 'true believers' then are psychologically able to murder civilians with a belief that such actions will receive a reward in the afterlife.

Interestingly, the Taliban has encountered difficulty in recruiting more members for its cause from its own territory of Afghanistan. There are reports of Taliban soldiers entering villages to recruit new members and being forced to leave after encountering mass armed uprisings of villagers.

FOCUS ON THE TALIBAN

AFGHANISTAN AND CENTRAL ASIA

Since the September 11, 2001 attacks on the World Trade Center and the Pentagon, significant scrutiny has fallen on Osama bin Laden and his Al Qaeda terrorist organization. There has also been discussion of the country which Osama bin Laden now calls home, Afghanistan, and the Taliban regime which administers 90% of it. But Afghanistan remains an enigma to many; what is its history? How did the Taliban come to power? How does Afghanistan relate to its neighbors, such as Pakistan, China, Iran and former Soviet republics? What do Afghans think of the U.S., and how difficult would it be to wage a war against terrorism there?

Twenty years of war has left Afghanistan shattered, destitute and in chaos. During the Cold War, the Soviet Union sought to exert its influence over this state on its southern border, and worked to install an allied communist regime in the capital, Kabul. Yet this government encountered strong opposition from mujihadeen rebels, and in 1979, the Soviet Union launched a massive invasion to crush the rebels and prevent the fall of the communist regime there.

At the beginning of the war, the U.S.S.R. had significant technological superiority; their attack helicopters and fighter-bombers owned the skies, and their army was stronger both in numbers and in armor. However, Soviet forces quickly discovered the challenges facing them: difficult and forbidding mountainous terrain to which the opposing Afghan rebels were accustomed, a lack of 'essential' targets for Soviet aircraft to strike, and a fiercely determined opposition force defending its own soil. Soon, the U.S. was supplying the mujihadeen rebels with arms and training, including the lethally effective Stinger anti-aircraft missiles. These missiles brought down hundreds of Soviet aircraft and forced them to fly high above battlefields, significantly reducing their effectiveness.

After ten agonizing years of conflict which pulled the drain plug on the Soviet economy and destroyed its army's morale, in February of 1989, they decided to withdraw their forces and end the 'Soviet Vietnam.'

Once the U.S.S.R. had departed, the U.S. considered its job finished, and abandoned interest in the area. Much of Afghanistan had been reduced to rubble, one million Afghans were dead, and there was no stable

government in place.

A horribly bloody civil war ensued, with the victorious mujihadeen, who were composed of the majority Pushtun population from central and south Afghanistan, making a grab for power against other ethnic groups who represented northern Afghan populations: Hazara, Tajik, Turkmen, and Uzbek. Neighboring countries sensed the power vacuum and attempted to influence events. The number of these neighboring countries increased when the Soviet Union fell apart in 1991; new sovereign republics were born to the north of Afghanistan, including Tajikistan, Turkmenistan and Uzbekistan.

This type of ethnic and sectarian violence was new to Afghanistan. The country is over 90% Sunni Muslim, with smaller ethnic groups such as Tajiks belonging to the minority Shiite sect. Although always conservative, Afghanistan's practice of Islam historically was tolerant and accepting of all religions and different cultures. Minority non-Sunni Muslims, Hindus, Jews and Sikhs lived together in peace in many cities and towns. Extreme orthodox interpretations of the Islamic faith did not exist in Afghanistan. The divisive politics and civil war of the early 1990s shattered this peaceful interaction, turning Islam from a force for peace and cultural understanding into an instrument to be used by those seeking power. Crime soared, and local warlords emerged as de facto leaders in a broken society.

In 1994, a movement known as 'the Taliban,' which means 'the Students,' emerged from Pakistan, where members had been living as refugees during the war against the Soviets and the civil war. This movement promised to establish law and order based on Islamic Law and to disarm the bandits and warlords that were hoarding the few resources remaining in Afghanistan. The Taliban attracted members of the Pushtun population in droves, playing on their desperation. It achieved limited success in restricting the influence of warlords, and was welcomed by many. It masqueraded as a humble movement, and its ambition was not recongnized until 1996, when it captured the capital, Kabul, and began to impose harsh rules on its society.

The Taliban movement arose from an unfortunate blend of radical politics and a twisted interpretation of Islam by illiterate clerics. During the war against the Soviet Union, hundreds of thousands of Pushtun Afghans fled south across the border into Pakistan for refuge. Radical northern Pakistani politicians established an extreme, anti-Western political party called the Jamiat-ul-Ulema-e-Islam (JUI), which recruited young Pakistanis and Afghan refugees with political rhetoric and a misinterpretation of a branch of Sunni Islam called Deobandism. The JUI won power in Pakistan's 1993 national election, and developed close contacts with the Pakistani military.

Also during the Soviet-Afghan War, the CIA hoped to bolster the mujihadeen's forces against the Soviets by encouraging the idea of a global jihad, which would attract radical Muslims from all over the world to fight in the region. Northern Pakistan became a staging ground for these extreme, multi-national Islamic forces, and gave additional support for local radical interpretations of Islam. Saudi exile Osama bin Laden was one of these individuals.

Thus, in 1994, Afghan refugees returned to their homeland from Pakistan, armed, with fundamentalist comrades from Pakistan and other countries eager to join the fight to establish a new state on the foundations of their extreme political and religious views. In 1996, when they took control of Kabul, Osama bin Laden arrived as a 'guest' and endeared himself to the one-eyed leader of the Taliban, Mullah Omar. The reason he made friends so quickly is that he spent over $40 million of his own money to bribe warlords across the country and align them with the Taliban. He also attracted significant donations from the ultra-orthodox Wahhabi Islamic sect in Saudi Arabia, which consisted of members who had aided his previous efforts against the more moderate Saudi regime. This quickly consolidated the Taliban's power, and enabled it to launch a brutal offensive against ethnic minorities in the north of Afghanistan. In 1998, the Taliban made great inroads against the Northern Alliance resistance, which consists of ethnic Tajik, Turkmen and Uzbek Afghans, pushing them into the Hindu Kush mountain range in the extreme northeast corner of the country.

The Taliban regime is one of the most consistent violators of human rights in the world. Women have been stoned to death for leaving their homes without a male guardian, and men have been murdered for trimming their beards, which are viewed as symbols of religious devotion. One village doctor fled to Great Britain after a chilling episode when a gun was put in his hands and he was forced at gunpoint by Taliban soldiers to shoot six of his fellow villagers in the head for their 'blasphemous behavior.'

The general public in Afghanistan are not ardent Taliban supporters. In fact, they have never seen their leader, since he forbids photography and does not make public appearances. Many Afghans are actually well-disposed to the U.S. as a result of support during the war against the Soviet Union. Yet dissent within the Afghan regime is simply not permitted.

The enforcement of such fanatical rules has acted as a beacon for radical Muslims around the world who are eager to join the Taliban's fight against the Northern Alliance, or to train in camps run by figures such as bin Laden in order to raise the struggle to a global level by bringing it to their home countries. Regionally, Afghanistan has taken on the characteristics of a magnet drawing iron filings from the sand, polarizing the region by welcoming radicals from neighboring states who later return home to cause internal unrest and sow the seeds of fundamentalism within local populations.

Pakistan is perhaps in the most difficult position. It has forged a relationship with the Taliban because it, along with bin Laden's Al Qaeda terrorist network and the JUI, provides significant support to Pakistan's northeastern problem: Kashmir. Rebel Pakistani forces there are fighting for self-determination, hoping to wrench control of that territory from India, and the struggle is treated as a jihad by the Taliban and bin Laden. As such, Pakistan receives the help it needs to

carry on that struggle, although it edges towards a public relations disaster due to the increasing numbers of terrorist attacks in the region launched by bin Laden affiliates.

Yet Pakistan's support for the Taliban is causing a severe domestic split which threatens to tear the country apart. Its northern provinces have been overrun by Taliban-like political parties which have begun to impose similarly oppressive local versions of Islamic Law. These groups have also engaged in their own versions of ethnic cleansing, or in this case, 'sectarian cleansing,' by intimidating and murdering Pakistani Shiite Muslims living in the area. As the reach of these groups expands, it raises the frightening possibility of a civil war or a coup which could put a Taliban-style government in place in Pakistan - a country with nuclear weapons which would pose a serious threat to its neighbors, China and India - which also possess nuclear weapons.

The Taliban also poses a serious threat to its other neighbors. It has attracted radical Muslims from the former Soviet republics to its north who hope to convert Uzbekistan, Tajikistan, and Turkmenistan into fundamentalist Islamic states, and who have committed serious acts of terrorism within their borders. Some of these individuals have hid in Afghanistan as 'guests' and have actually assembled small armies, threatening to invade these small neighboring states. To the west, Iran considers the Taliban a threat. The Iranian government is Shiite Muslim, the group which the Taliban has been systematically slaughtering in Afghanistan. Some of the most extreme Sunni Muslim minorities in

Iran have taken refuge in Afghanistan and are being trained as terrorists against Iran by Osama bin Laden's group. The Taliban has already executed a number of Iranian diplomats, an act which almost led to war between the two states. To the east, the Taliban has been training and arming Muslim minority groups in China which have mounted military and terrorist attacks against Chinese security forces in the province of Xinjiang.

One final point should be made: the Taliban produces 75% of the world's heroin. It is also one of the world leaders in consumer goods smuggling due to its abusive use of a trade agreement with Pakistan. Heroin and goods smuggling constitute 90% of Afghanistan's economic output, and represent the only real employers outside of the five factories in the country. (There were over 200 factories in 1980.) The only solvent banks are operated by drug runners. The Taliban collects a substantial tax on heroin and smuggling, which is the only significant source of its budget. Although most of Osama bin Laden's bank accounts around the world have been frozen, he makes millions of dollars each year with his personal stake in the drug trade, which makes him more or less immune from overseas attempts to limit his personal finances.

FOCUS ON ISLAM

It cannot be stressed enough that the perpetrators of the attacks on September 11, 2001 were following a twisted and extreme interpretation of Islam which is not shared by the vast majority of the world's Islamic population. Although a brief summary will miss many important details and over-simplify others, it is useful to sketch a few very basic facts about Islam in order to gain a general understanding of the religion and to understand how the beliefs of the terrorists differed sharply from mainstream Islam.

Islam is the second-largest religion in the world after Christianity. Over one billion people are Muslim, and six million of those reside in the U.S. By 2050, Islam is projected to be the world's most-practiced religion. A Muslim is simply a follower of the religion of Islam. Islam was founded in the year 622 by Muhammed the Prophet, who lived from 570 to 632. Mecca (Saudi Arabia) is the holiest city of Islam, because it was there that the angel Gabriel revealed the first revelation to Muhammed in 610. In 622, Muhammed moved north to Medina (Islam's second-holiest city), on a 300 mile trek known as the hegira which is still replicated today, to escape persecution. There, Islam was firmly established. This trek also marked the beginning of the Muslim lunar calendar

By 750, Islam had spread west to parts of Spain and east as far as China. During the Crusades in the Middle Ages, most battles raged between Palestinian Jews and European Christians who were attempting to conquer Jerusalem. It was only when Christian Crusaders began to ravage the holy land of Arabia that their expulsion was decided upon. This expulsion, led by Saladin, was comparatively chivalrous and widely respected in Western Europe. The

---

Two words have been confused heavily in the Western media relating to Islam. First, the term 'jihad' is often taken to translate into 'holy war,' which is not always the case. Its literal interpretation is 'struggle,' and it is used by most Muslims to denote an internal, personal struggle in the sense of 'striving,' usually to live a better, more noble life.

---

exception was the fate which befell Reynald of Chatillon, the Christian leader of the Crusaders, who had raped and pillaged his way through Arabia; Saladin personally separated his head from his body.

By 1550, tensions in Western Europe had increased and wars broke out which resulted in the expulsion of Muslims from Spain and other sections of Europe. Today, the densest Muslim population lies between the western coast of Africa and the Philippines. Africa represents the largest area of expansion of the religion today. 'Muslim' is not synonymous with 'Arab.' Arab describes the group of people whose ethnic roots can be traced to the Arabian region; there are Arab Jews and Arab Christians in addition to Arab Muslims. Arabic is the language of Islam because it is the language of Islam's holy book, the Qu'ran. But followers of Islam do not necessarily have Arabic as a first language, given that Islam is practiced worldwide.

Islam is closely related to Judaism and Christianity. Muslims recognize a series of prophets who came before Muhammed, including Abraham, David, Moses and Jesus. In Islam, Muhammed simply had the 'final word.' Christian and Muslim doctrine generally agree on some important ideas about Jesus' life, including the concept of miraculous birth, and his abilities to cure illnesses and raise the dead. Muslim doctrine does not, however, generally hold that Jesus was killed during his crucifixion; rather, it holds that he escaped and reappeared to his disciples without first having died.

There are two main texts in Islam: the Qu'ran and the Hadith. The Qu'ran are the words of God as revealed to Muhammed, which constitute the essential text of Islam. The Hadith is a collection of Mohammad's sayings, which is considered more as a guide to living.

A Muslim's duties are described in the Five Pillars of Islam. These are: first, to recite at least once during her lifetime the shahadah the holy creed: "There is no God but God and Muhammed is his Prophet"). Second, to perform the salat (prayer) five times daily. This is performed while facing in the direction of Mecca in the morning, at noon, mid-afternoon, sunset, and bedtime. Third, to donate to charity via the zakat, a form of charity tax. Fourth, to fast during daylight hours in the month of Ramadan, which is believed to be the month that Muhammed received the first revelation of the Qu'ran. Fifth, to make at least one hajj (pilgrimage) to Mecca, if financially and physically possible.

Common beliefs include a belief in Heaven and Hell, forgiveness of sins, and the existence of a Devil which drives people to sin. Other common beliefs include a rejection of alcohol, drugs, gambling and the eating of pork.

Originally, Islamic states did not distinguish between religious and civil law, although in the 20th century, some states such as Turkey have made the transition to secular law and government. Afghanistan under the Taliban regime is certainly not the only state to be ruled by Islamic Law, but it is by far the most extreme, radically conservative interpretation of that law.

Oftentimes, reference is made to different sects of Islam. There are three different sects which represent the main divisions. The first sect consists of Sunni

Muslims, who constitute 90% of all Muslims. They are usually considered to be mainstream traditionalists, and have had great success adapting to different national cultures and living in secular societies. Shiite Muslims constitute a small but important minority of Muslims who split from the Sunni sect due to an ancient dispute about the successor to Muhammed. The Shiite sect usually involves a more strict and conservative interpretation of Islam, and includes a belief in 12 heavenly Imams (perfect teachers) who led the Shiites after Muhammed. There is also a mystical sect known as Sufism which emphasizes personal interaction with God through meditation, and which borrows from Buddhism and Christianity. Nevertheless, Islam does not have denominational mosques.

Two words have been confused heavily in the Western media relating to Islam. First, the term 'jihad' is often taken to translate into 'holy war,' which is not always the case. Its literal interpretation is 'struggle,' and it is used by most Muslims to denote an internal, personal struggle in the sense of 'striving,' usually to live a better, more noble life. The word is also used to describe the idea of holy war in the sense of defending Islam against non-Muslims, but it must be remembered

that this is not the common usage.

Also, the word 'Fundamentalist' is sometimes associated with 'terrorist,' which is an abusive interpretation of the term. Although the word is often used loosely, fundamentalist Islam is more akin to 'conservative Islam' in that fundamentalists strictly follow Islamic rules, promote the general idea of Islamic Law, and probably view the West as secular and decadent. Yet terrorist groups which invoke Islam for their foundation constitute the extreme, radical fringe of fundamentalists. The distinction is in the belief held by terrorists and the Taliban that Islamic Law must be imposed in its most rigid sense without a choice, and with violence if needed. This is not a belief held by most fundamentalists.

The Taliban regime and terrorists in groups such as Al Qaeda actually have little knowledge of the teachings of Islam, Islamic history or Afghan history. There is no opportunity for education, either, because dissent and discussion is not permitted. The Taliban movement originated from the more mainstream Sunni sect, but relies on radical and extreme misinterpretations of limited sections of the Qu'ran. On a very basic level, the Qu'ran forbids the killing of innocent people, as well as the killing of other Muslims, two prohibitions that the Taliban regime has trampled time and time again. Although the movement and the Al Qaeda terrorist organization are both predicated on Islam, there is no question that it is a distorted version which is not representative of the Islam practiced by the vast majority of the world's Muslims.

TERRORISM IN AFRICA

Africa hosted the birth of modern post-war terrorism en route to the so-called 'third wave' of decolonization in the 1950s and 1960s. Disenfranchised groups seeking self-determination and independence from colonial powers such as Britain, France and Belgium used terrorism as a prime tactic in wearing down the resolve of their colonial oppressors. Since then, terrorism has been used as a destabilizing tactic by groups hoping to grab power and overthrow regimes, and has also been used widely in the course of bloody ethnic and tribal conflicts in central Africa.

Most terrorism in Africa, as in the rest of the world, has domestic goals such as separation or overthrow, and many states in Africa have been dealing with the problem of domestic terrorism for decades. Nevertheless, sometimes domestic African terrorist groups attack foreign nationals for political publicity. In Angola, for example of a separatist group, the National Union for the Total Independence of Angola (UNITA) has been known to kidnap Western foreigners, attack humanitarian convoys and shoot down civilian airplanes. Similar examples of separatist violence can be found in Ethiopia, Somalia and Eritrea among others.

Terrorism often takes place in the wider context of civil strife and violence, and is frequently employed simply as a tactic of war by groups hoping to gain control of the government of a country. Sierra Leone has faced disturbing examples of this type of violence against civilians in recent years, particularly during and after the Revolutionary United Front's siege of the capital, Freetown. Smaller militant groups like the Armed Forces Revolutionary Council (AFRC) have held civilians, peacekeepers and UN observers hostage and demanded political compromises and the release of prisoners.

Ethnic and tribal terrorism can be found in central Africa, especially in the region of the Democratic Republic of Congo (DRC), Uganda and Rwanda. Members of the Hutu and Tutsi tribes have been vying for control of the governments of all three countries, and in the wake of the bloodbaths of the early 1990s in Rwanda and the DRC, terrorist attacks occur sporadically. The most famous recent example was an attack in which Rwandan Hutus attacked three tourist camps, kidnapping 14 tourists and slaughtering 8 of them including two U.S. citizens, four British citizens and two New Zealanders. Ethnic terrorism has also occurred in Nigeria in the context of battles over control of prosperous oil-producing regions in an otherwise impoverished country. Some attacks have included the kidnapping of foreign oil workers.

Terrorism is conducted by the state in a number of African countries, most notably Zimbabwe. President Robert Mugabe's ruling Zanu-PF party regularly terrorizes Zimbabweans, and ensures electoral victory before each election through hostage-takings, torture and 'disappearances' of opposition party members. Mugabe has also used so called 'war veterans' to attack and intimidate white farmers in order to force them to give their land to the state.

Islamic terrorism is most commonly associated with north Africa, although notable examples can be found of Islamic militant groups terrorizing local targets in other parts of the continent, such as Qibla in South Africa and the Allied Democratic Forces in Uganda. The most important four African states with Islamic terrorist groups are Egypt, Algeria, Sudan, and Libya.

Egypt is a moderate Islamic state and an important U.S. ally. It is also home to a number of militant Islamic terrorist groups which target the Egyptian government for its rather conciliatory attitude to Israel and its friendship with the U.S., as well as international targets. The most notable two groups are Al-Gama'a al-Islamiyya (The Islamic Group) and the Jihad Group (Islamic Jihad). Both groups have members who have trained at Al Qaeda camps in Afghanistan. Al-Gama'a al-Islamiyya declared a cease-fire in 1999 after Egyptian authorities arrested a number of important members. Nevertheless, the group is still in existence, and is known world-wide for its precise execution of machine gun attacks on tourists. Its stated goal has been to ruin the Egyptian economy by destroying the tourist trade, thus forcing concessions in the form of a tougher policy towards the U.S. and

Israel. On April 18, 1996, members of that group killed 18 and wounded 17 Greek tourists, mistaking them for Israeli citizens, in a machine gun attack outside a Cairo hotel. The four terrorists in that case escaped, and may have fled the country. On November 13, 1997, the group killed three in a machine gun attack on a tourist train 500 miles south of Cairo. Four days later, six members of the same group launched a machine gun attack at the ancient archaeological site in Luxor in a widely-publicized event which killed 63 foreign civilians and injured 26. The six terrorists in that case were later killed in a shoot-out with Egyptian authorities.

Algeria has suffered staggering numbers of civilian casualties at the hands of Islamic terrorists. Algeria won its independence from France in July, 1962 after an eight-year revolutionary war. In 1992, when the dictator President Chadli resigned, Al Qaeda members returned to their homeland from Afghanistan and attempted to cause a fundamentalist Islamic revolution with a violent terror campaign in conjunction with over 50 other militant Islamic groups. With seed money from Osama bin Laden, the Al Qaeda members helped establish the Armed Islamic Group (GIA), which proceeded to engage in the wholesale slaughter of Algerian civilians. In a four-year period, over 110,000 civilians were killed by

constant terror attacks which included the GIA's use of enormous car bombs in marketplaces, airports and bus terminals that would spread severed limbs more than a quarter-mile from the blast site. The GIA and other groups received funding from the government of Iran, which led to Algeria severing diplomatic ties with Iran in 1993. These groups also received funding from private citizens outside Algeria who were sympathetic to the cause, most of whom were living in France. A few of these individuals living in France also had independent ties to the Al Qaeda network. The GIA and similar groups still operate in Algeria today.

Sudan and Libya are Africa's two

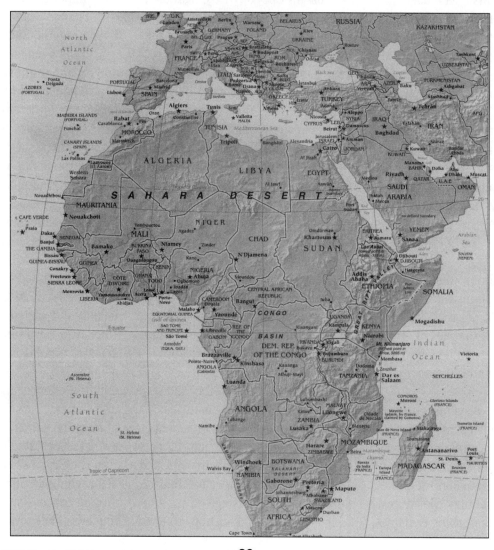

states which sponsor international terrorism. Sudan, on Egypt's southern border, offers safe haven to members of a number of terrorist organizations, including Hezb'allah, Abu Nidal, Hamas, Palestinian Islamic Jihad, Al-Gama'a al-Islamiyya and Al Qaeda. Sudan facilitates the funding of these organizations, permitting them access to liquid bank accounts, the opportunity to operate fund-raising businesses, and the occasion to receive donations from private individuals and governments such as Iran. It supports militant Islamic opposition groups in Egypt, Algeria, Uganda, Tunisia, Ethiopia, and Eritrea. Although Sudan eventually complied with U.S. requests that it expel Osama bin Laden from its territory in 1996, it continues to harbor other accused terrorists despite UN Security Council resolutions which demand their extradition. Specifically, Sudan is protecting three members of Al-Gama'a al-Islamiyya who attempt-ed to assassinate Egyptian President Hosni Mubarak in Ethiopia in 1995.

The Libyan government and its embarrassing leader, Col. Muammar Qaddafi, have sponsored terrorism since the 1970s, and offer an interesting comparison to the Taliban regime of today. Qaddafi was raised on the 'pan-Arabic' rhetoric of Egyptian leader Gamal Abdel Nasser in the 1950s, who promoted a revolu-tionary vision of Arab nationalism and unity, particularly on causes such as opposition to Israel. When Qaddafi took power in a relatively bloodless coup in September of 1969 which was known as 'The September Revolution,' he attempted to become the pre-eminent leader of the Arab world by trying to assemble a coalition of Arab leaders who could agree on important Middle East policies. But his timing was unfortunate; he was left out of the loop by the leaders of Egypt, Syria and Saudi Arabia during the October 1973 war with Israel, and was unable to prevent Egypt and Syria from entering into direct peace negotiations with Israel following that conflict. An embittered Qaddafi's vision of a united Arab world was crumbling, and he turned to alternative means to try to promote his more radical view of how Arab states should behave.

He exploited the Cold War to get funding from the Soviet Union and created an annual terrorism budget of $600 million. Libya became the 'Afghanistan' of the 1980s, insofar as over 8,000 foreign terrorists would gravitate to its territory for training in camps each year. He trained his own government agents for terrorist actions as well, and ordered more and more audacious attacks which eventually led to his alienation. In one example, he ordered his agents to kill Egyptian President Hosni Mubarak in the mid-1980s; when their attempts failed, he had his naval forces place mines in front of the entrance to the Suez Canal in the Red Sea. His agents helped plan the bombing of the West Berlin nightclub, La Belle, which killed three U.S. soldiers and wounded 80 in addition to the over 200 German civilian victims. In response to this and three other terrorist attacks in Europe, in 1986 the U.S. bombed military targets in Libya as well as Qaddafi's house, killing his baby daughter.

In 1989, Qaddafi's agents participated in the bombing of Pan Am Flight 103 over Lockerbie, Scotland, possibly with assistance from the Iranian government. When Libya refused to hand the suspects over to U.S. or British authorities for the purpose of prosecution, the UN Security Council imposed a punishing set of sanctions on the country which made it difficult for Libya to make money off of its one central asset: oil. With the concurrent end of the Cold War, Libya's money stream dried up, and it eventually extradited the suspects for trial. Although Qaddafi's blustering rhetoric has not ceased, no one pays any attention to it anymore. Indeed, Libya's support for terrorism seems to be nearing an end in order to end its ostracism from the rest of the world.

The central economic difference between Libya and Afghanistan is that while Libya makes a substantial portion of its money from legitimate oil sales and has a functioning econ-omy as a result, Afghanistan makes most of its money from heroin and opium sales and goods smuggling. It already has a broken economy, and the abject poverty of its inhabitants is a continuing feature. Such a difference suggests that sanctions which appeared to work against Libya will probably not work against Afghanistan. Military action may be successful in the short term, but one of the main challenges to the West will be to repair and reform Afghanistan's devastated economy and cancerous black market in the long term.

TERRORISM IN THE MIDDLE EAST

Terrorism gripped the Middle East for almost the entire 20th century, and does not show signs of abating in the 21st century. Most of it has been focused on the question of Israel, although it has expanded to address the policies of Arab states as well. The Middle East has also evolved to become the region with the longest history of state-sponsored terrorism. The states we will consider here are Lebanon, Syria, Iran, Iraq, Saudi Arabia, Jordan, Yemen and Israel and Palestine. In this field, Lebanon is associated most strongly with its well-known terrorist group, Hezb'allah (Party of God).

Hezb'allah was founded in 1982 by a group of militant Shiite Muslims in Lebanon who had as their goal the removal of foreign elements from Lebanese soil and the establishment of a fundamentalist Islamic regime which would rule Lebanon under Islamic Law. As Iran had just experienced a revolution in 1979 which installed a fundamentalist Shiite regime led by Ayatollah Khomeni, it was eager to provide financing and support to encourage Hezb'allah's project. The conditions were already ripe for the formation of such a

group, given the ongoing battles between Lebanese Muslims and Lebanese Christians, and the involvement of U.S. and French forces in the disputes. But the primary reason Hezb'allah was founded specifically in the year 1982 was because it was the year Israel invaded Lebanon for the second time (the first was 1978). As a consequence, Hezb'allah held as its initial goal the ejection of Israeli (and U.S.) forces from Lebanon. It rejoiced on May 22, 2000 when Israel finally withdrew its occupation, but did not consider its task complete, since it swore to oppose Israeli occupation of the

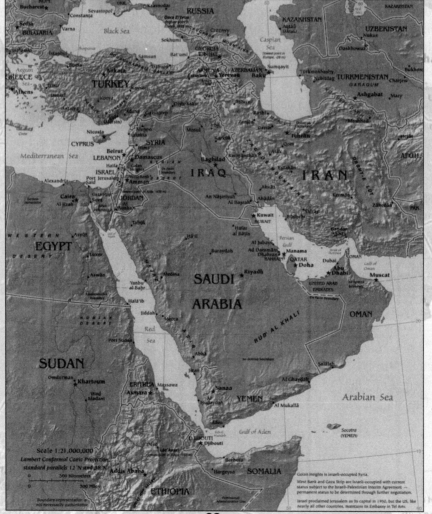

West Bank and Gaza Strip, and because it had not accomplished its goal of installing a fundamentalist Islamic regime in Lebanon. Hezb'allah still receives funding from Iran, and is still active.

Syria is still considered a state sponsor of terrorism, although its activities are not on the scale of earlier decades. It was one of the original countries to be placed on the U.S. State Department's list of state sponsors of terrorism when that list was started in 1979, and has remained on it ever since. Syria still provides safe haven for members of a number of terrorist groups, including the PKK, Palestinian Islamic Jihad, and Hizb'allah. The Palestinian group Hamas even has a set of offices in Damascus. But although it harbours terrorists, it does not appear that Syria has been involved in the planning of terrorist attacks since 1986, and sometimes it has used its influence to restrain these groups' activities. This could be related to the fact that Syria was an ally of the Soviet Union during the Cold War, and that its relationship with Western countries was improving by 1986. Syria participated in the allied coalition against Iraq, although this has led some to believe that secret deals were struck which would help Syria in other ways. President Hafez al-Asad has led Syria since 1970, and will probably not change his policies offering safe haven to anti-Israeli terrorists much more until Israel withdraws its forces from Syrian soil. Israel invaded Syria in 1967, taking over the Golan Heights and forcing over 100,000 Syrians out of their homes, and still occupies

that territory. But there is at least the possibility that Syria could be an ally for the U.S. in its campaign against terrorism in Afghanistan.

Iran is the unquestioned world leader in state-sponsored terrorism. Although Afghanistan may be a rival in this regard, Iran is a much more populated state which has more funds to devote to terrorism. Ever since a fundamentalist Shiite Muslim regime took power in 1979 with Ayatollah Khomeni at the top of the totem pole, Iran has supported and funded terrorist groups and engaged in domestic and international assassination attempts. When President Khatami was elected to power in May 1997, observers in the West hoped it would herald the beginning of a change in policy. Yet despite his moderate political views and condemnation of terrorism, Iranian policies have only changed slightly.

This is because the current Ayatollah, as religious leader, commands a group of more radical followers who are not likely to change their views on the subject of terrorism regardless of the instructions of the President. Iran's policies have improved only insofar as Iran no longer uses its own agents to plan and commit terrorist acts. But it still funds, trains and arms terrorist groups such as its Shiite favorite, Hezb'allah, as well as Sunni Muslim groups such as the PFLP, the GIA, Islamic Jihad, and al-Gama'a al-Islamiyya. Given Iran's revolutionary regime, it is interesting that it sacrifices its ideals by supporting Sunni Muslim groups, especially the last three groups which are part of the Osama bin Laden network in Afghanistan, Iran's neighbor and enemy. Afghanistan and Iran almost went to war in 1998 when the Taliban beheaded a group of important

Iranian diplomats, but it seems the two countries can put their differences aside when it comes to supporting terrorist groups. The challenge for the West will be to figure out if there is a way to help increase the power of President Khatami at the expense of the more conservative elements of power in Tehran in order to arrive at a substantial change in policy.

Saddam Hussein's regime in Iraq is also considered to be a state sponsor of terrorism. It provides sanctuary to members of a number of terrorist organizations, including the PKK, the Palestine Liberation Front, and Abu Nidal. The regime also plans terror attacks with its own agents, including attacks on international targets, UN relief workers and prominent politicians. One recent example was the plot to assassinate U.S. President George Bush during a visit to Kuwait. Iraq regularly gives money to suicide bombing operations launched by Palestinians in Israel. Evidence suggests that Iraq assisted with the 1993 World Trade Center bombing by offering technical advice to Al Qaeda terrorists on the manufacture of the bomb, and may have assisted with several bombings in Saudi Arabia. There is also evidence that Osama bin Laden was in contact with the Iraqi government from his base in Afghanistan during the week prior to the September 11 attacks in the United States. Saddam Hussein also uses mass-scale terrorism against his own people. He attacked the ethnic Kurdish population in northern Iraq with chemical weapons and bombs, killing thousands.

Saudi Arabia and Jordan are two of the United States' biggest allies in the Middle East. Saudi

Arabia's ruling royal family faces dissent from inside as well as from outside due to its policies towards the U.S. and Israel. One of Osama bin Laden's central complaints is the presence of U.S. military forces on Saudi soil. Some extreme Islamic groups within Saudi Arabia offer funding to bin Laden's organization, although the Saudi government is active in preventing it, and generally executes those who are caught. Jordan has also helped take the lead in prosecuting terrorists in the region. Jordan faces terrorist attacks due to its moderate policy towards Israel and the U.S. King Abdullah's administration has been vigilant in tracking down and prosecuting accused terrorists within its territory.

Yemen is known as a potential safe haven for terrorists, and is another important operating location for bin Laden's Al Qaeda organization. Marxist South Yemen merged with conservative North Yemen over a decade ago, and since then, the country has seen a number of terrorist bombings and hostage-takings. The central question in Yemen is whether President Ali Abdullah Saleh can control crime in a country with rabidly independent tribes and an average of three guns per citizen. Yemen is a global clearing house for the illegal arms trade, and in certain areas, is considered relatively lawless. After the bombing of the USS Cole in Aden, Yemen, only more questions were raised about the Yemeni government's willingness and ability to take the steps necessary to stamp out terrorism in its territory.

Israel and Palestine have been the location of terrorism since the beginning of the 20th century. After the 1917 Balfour Declaration, when Britain decided to establish a 'homeland' for Jews in Palestine, civil strife became a permanent feature of life in the area. Palestinians resented this trend of resettling, and believed their land was being taken from them, whereas Zionist Jews believed it was not only their right to settle there, but that they should be accorded statehood and the right to self-govern. Terrorist actions from each party were launched against the other, and radical Zionist groups

Yemen is known as a potential safe haven for terrorists, and is another important operating location for bin Laden's Al Qaeda organization.

such as Irgun and the Stern Gang launched terror attacks against the British forces which administered the region. In fact, two prominent Israeli terrorists of that age, the leader of Irgun, Menachem Begin, and one of the leaders of the Stern Gang, Yitzhak Shamir, both became prime ministers of Israel, just as the leader of the Palestinian Liberation Organization (PLO), Yasser Arafat, continued as leader of the Palestinian Authority.

The modern era of terrorism in the Israel-Palestine region began after the 1967 Six-Day War, when Israel attacked Egypt and Syria, took possession of sections of their countries, and occupied the Palestinian West Bank of the Jordan River. What followed was the rapid organization of a number of Islamic and Arab-based terrorist groups whose goal was to end Israeli occupation of Palestine. The conflict has continued ever since, with untold innocent lives lost and property damaged. Israel has pursued a policy of government assassination, which has delegitimized in the eyes of many, while claiming such actions are necessary to counter the brutal terror attacks launched by Palestinian terrorist groups such as Palestinian Islamic Jihad, Hamas, and Fatah, as well as the Lebanese group Hezb'allah.

One of the central difficulties with Palestine is a common one in the Islamic Middle East: if too many concessions appear to be made to Israel by Palestinian leaders such as Yasser Arafat, more radical Islamic groups may target the Palestinian Authority in addition to Israel. Thus, the room for negotiation is less than would be expected, and the opportunities for peace are limited by the more militant terrorist factions. To address the problems in this area requires careful, sensitive steps towards the center, probably mediated by a third party, which is to say nothing of the almost intractable problem of assigning administrative control over contested parts of Jerusalem. Although Palestine is self-administered today, these larger questions such as the 'Jerusalem Question' will have to be resolved before an agreed-upon declaration of Palestinian statehood can occur. If this can be accomplished, and it is perceived as fair by both sides, it is likely terrorism in the region will diminish.

TERRORISM IN EUROPE

Although Europe does not differ from other regions in that it also faces terrorist threats, it has experienced great success with regional cooperation in locating and arresting suspected terrorists. Like the rest of the world, Europe's problems with terrorism are primarily domestic. The main states which should be considered are the United Kingdom, Spain, France, Germany, Italy, Greece, Turkey and Russia. Although Albania and Kosovo have experienced terrorist acts on a wide scale, they have occurred in the context of a war, and should be considered war crimes in most instances.

The United Kingdom's experience with terrorism is perhaps the most interesting in Europe, and stems from hundreds of years of tumultuous history with Ireland. In the 1300s, English forces overran much of Ireland, pushing the Irish tribes to the fringe of their island. Following years saw successive English monarchs sending nobles to Ireland to take land into their possession. In England, by 1600, successive monarchs decided whether to follow Henry VIII's Protestant Church of England, or the traditional Catholic church which had been inherited from Norman conquerors who overran England from France in 1066. This split was problematic for England, but would prove debilitating for parts of Ireland. Although most of Ireland remained loyal to Catholic King

James II of the late 1600s, in the 1700s, followers of William of Orange attempted to establish Protestant control over northern parts of Ireland. In 1800, English Prime Minister William Pitt initiated the Act of Unity, which consolidated Scotland and Ireland into a Parliament 'for the British.' But only Protestant men were permitted to represent Ireland for almost 30 years.

World War I brought tensions in Ireland to the boil, with Catholics furious both at contradictions in English policy and at Protestant attempts to remain united with England. By 1915, weapons were flowing in from Germany, which wanted to cause a distracting problem for its enemy, and money was flowing in from the United States, where Irish immigrants sent what money they could muster back to Catholic nationalist movements like Sinn Fein. Led by Michael Collins, Irish nationalists engaged in shadowy warfare against English forces on Irish soil, and in 1922, the Irish state was born in a compromise solution which kept the six 'Ulster' counties of Northern Ireland, which had majority Protestant populations who wanted to remain united with Britain, under English control.

This has formed the source of today's terrorist attacks, with minority Catholics in Northern Ireland hoping to wear down the resolve of the British to remain in the region and thus reunite Ulster with its southern neighbor. This case is a good example of the power of

mythology, with radical members of Catholic political parties such as Sinn Fein invoking the memory of Michael Collins for motivation (even though Collins' forces rarely attacked non military targets), and Protestants hearkening back to the 18th century with the names of groups such as the Orangemen, following the tradition of William of Orange.

Modern terrorism began around 1969 in Northern Ireland, and a steady supply of weapons to the Irish Republican Army (Catholic) turned it into an urban war. After twenty years of violence in Northern Ireland and the British mainland, both sides agreed it was in their interest to pursue a peace agreement. This was finally secured in 1994, but it fell apart in 1996 when two massive Republican bombs hit the Canary Wharf business center in London and gutted the center of the city of Manchester. Since 1969, terrorism related to Northern Ireland has killed 3,500 civilians, injured over 30,000, destroyed hundreds of millions of pounds worth of property, killed 300 police officers (Royal Ulster Constabulary) and injured 9,000 more.

Today, there are radical groups on both the Republican (Catholic) side and the Loyalist or Unionist (Protestant) side. With the Irish Republican Army (IRA) moving into the mainstream during peace negotiations, splinter groups such as the Real IRA have assumed the mantle of terrorist attacks in an ongoing and brutal way. Their primary targets have been civilians in crowded pubs and other civilian targets in London as well as in Northern Ireland. Although Loyalist fringe groups such as the Orange Volunteers formed to 'fight fire with fire,' it is generally acknowledged that the bulk of terrorism comes from the Republican side. Part of the difficulty today is that even after the Good Friday Agreement of April 1998, disagreements abound over how to 'decommission' the huge stockpile of weapons that the IRA has amassed over the years. The other part of the difficulty has been the decision to decommission some weapons in exchange for the granting of amnesty to imprisoned Republican terrorists who in some cases were responsible for the murders of hundreds of women and children. Treating them as 'prisoners of war' who could be released was a controversial decision which still arouses rancor in many segments of the British populace.

The case of Northern Ireland is also an interesting example because it offers a case where the United States has harbored terrorists and permitted the funding of

terrorist groups operating in another country. Because of the powerful 'Irish Lobby' in the U.S. which put pressure on the U.S. Government to support the cause of Northern Ireland Republicans, when terrorists were accused of crimes in Britain, they would flee to the U.S. and would be given safe haven. This practice ended in the mid-1980s when it became clear that this policy was blatantly self-contradictory with U.S. requests that other countries hand over suspected terrorists to it. But the problem of private financing of terrorism in Northern Ireland from sources in the U.S. continues. The U.S. should seriously consider ending this hypocritical posture if it hopes to have any success in convincing other countries to clamp down on foreign terrorism

financing in their own territories.

Europe also is home to other examples of terrorism that stem from ethnic groups being incorporated into larger states, and then fighting for independence from them. In northeast Spain on the Atlantic coast, Basque separatists have been fighting for independence since 1959. The terrorist group Euskadi ta Askatasuna (ETA, 'Basque Fatherland and Liberty') has committed most of its terrorist acts following the death of dictator President Franco in 1975. This raises interesting questions of why ETA would increase its terrorism in years when civil and political freedoms were being extended across the country, and when the Basque provinces were being given high levels of autonomy. Convincing explanations for this are hard to find.

Russia experienced an increase in terrorist attacks in the 1990s, largely coming from ethnic Chechens from the Caucasus region of southwest Russia. Chechnya was conquered by Stalin, who ejected many Chechens and forced

ethnic Russians to settle in the area in order to assimilate it into the U.S.S.R. Although later allowed to resettle in their homeland, Chechens have historically borne a grudge against Moscow. When the Soviet Union fell apart in 1991 and formerly Soviet republics gained independence, Chechens were among a number of ethnic groups which demanded but were denied independence. Chechnya's attempts to secede were met with a Russian invasion in 1994; this First Chechen War lasted until 1996, when Russian forces were defeated and forced to withdraw after a peace agreement was reached. At the conclusion of this brutal civil war, some radical Chechen groups launched terror attacks in Moscow and other locations with the ultimate goal of winning independence, but also for revenge against the atrocities and war crimes committed by some of the Russian soldiers in the First Chechen War. In 1999, Russia launched a second, crushing invasion under the pretext of hunting Chechen 'terrorists,' although the scale of the assault made it clear that Russia was avenging its defeat in the first war. It obliterated the Chechen capital, Groznyy, occupied Chechnya, and now faces sporadic terrorist attacks as a result.

Turkey faces ethnic terrorism from the Kurdistan Worker's Party (PKK), which represents ethnic Kurds who have been campaigning for the creation of a separate and independent state of Kurdistan out of parts of eastern Turkey and northern Iraq. This is the same ethnic group whose civilians were attacked with bombs and chemical weapons by Saddam Hussein in northern Iraq, which is the major justification for the northern no-fly zone enforced by the U.S. over Iraq.

Germany's main terrorist organization is the Red Army Faction (RAF), which was formerly known as the Baader-Meinhof Gang. During the 1960s and 1970s, this group committed a number of terrorist acts against West Germany and against U.S. military bases there. Although the RAF had a left-wing/socialist ideology, its actions also stemmed from the disillusionment of youth in the post-World War II era. The group officially disbanded in 1998, so its current status is unknown. Germany's more immediate threat comes from right-wing racist 'skinhead' groups, which have been known to attack foreigners and ethnic minorities, particularly in the poorer areas of eastern Germany. Italy has a similar history with left-wing violence like the RAF; in this case it was the Red Brigades. This group, which was founded by students in 1969, was responsible for political violence until it went dormant in 1988. Some former members have formed a new organization, however, called the Territorial Nuclei, which committed low-level violence against U.S. interests in Italy during the NATO bombing campaign against Serbia.

Greece has been described as Europe's 'weakest link' in combating terrorism due to its apathetic law enforcement approach and lack of police intelligence capabilities. Its primary terrorist group is 17 November, a radical left-wing group founded in 1975 and named for a famous November 1973 student uprising against the then-ruling military regime. It uses rocket attacks, bombings and drive-by moped shootings in order to promote its agenda, which is against the Greek government, Turkey, NATO, the U.S. military's presence in Greece, and the European Union. Although its attacks have not generally produced mass casualties, many European states find the frequency of those attacks disturbing.

France has experienced the most problems with international radical Islamic terrorism in Europe as a result of its old colonial connections to North Africa. A faction of the Algerian GIA is operating within France, and helps to orchestrate terrorist attacks within Algeria as well as within France. French officials have arrested several members of this group who have been to Al Qaeda training camps in Afghanistan. France has endured serious terrorist attacks by these Algerian groups, including one attack on the Paris Metro, which prompted officials to supplement police security with military personnel at key potential targets such as Metro and train stations. Also, because France borders on the south with Basque counties in Spain, it finds ETA members often hiding in its territory. France and Spain have come to extensive agreements on close cooperation in order to track down and capture ETA terror suspects.

If one lesson can be learned from Europe, it is the building of mutual trust over the years which has enabled extensive intelligence sharing and cooperation on apprehending terrorists. If this type of cooperation can be replicated on a global level, law enforcement officials in countries around the world will be in a much better position to clamp down on international terrorist organizations.

TERRORISM IN LATIN AMERICA

Terrorism in Latin America is often conducted by left-wing students in the course of a guerilla conflict with their government. In some cases, it has produced clear results for the terrorist organizations. There are three countries or areas which deserve attention: Colombia, Peru and the so-called 'Tri-border' region where Argentina, Brazil and Paraguay meet.

Columbia is home to the Fuerzas Armadas Revolucionarias de Colombia (Revolutionary Armed Forces of Colombia, FARC) and the Ejercito de Liberacion Nacional (National Liberation Army, ELN). These guerilla groups were started in the mid-1960s by students who hoped to impose Marxist ideology on poor, rural areas of their country. They brought a semblance of law and order to areas which rarely saw the Colombian government, set up protection networks for cocaine producers to receive a steady income, and then focused on the Colombian government.

Today, FARC and the ELN have gained so much power that their peace process with the government will likely permit them to administer certain sections of the country. FARC has begun to send representatives to international governmental conventions. Yet FARC and the ELN continue terrorism, primarily to raise funds and financially hurt the government. Their tactics involve kidnapping foreign citizens ranging from children to high-ranking oil executives in order to receive ransoms and scare away companies. They target infrastructure and foreign energy companies, and extort money with what is known as 'FARC Law 002,' a 'tax' on entities worth more than $1 million. In 2000, FARC attempted to destroy a major U.S. coal firm for not paying its 'tax,' and one of the largest crude oil pipelines in Colombia was attacked a total of 152 times.

Peru faces a smaller terrorist threat than Colombia, though from a brutal organization. In an example which probably should be hidden from undergraduates and law students, the Sendero Luminoso (Shining Path) organization was started by a bitter and revolutionary-minded university study group. Like the Colombian groups, Sendero gained inspiration from the Cuban revolution, but also from their activist professor. They decided to try to implement their vision of Marxism in real life by launching terror attacks, hoping for a violent and oppressive government response which they anticipated would cause a general public revolt.

As in Colombia, they gained support among the rural poor; their favored tactics included murdering wealthy

landowners and distributing their property among the peasants. They established a rigid structure to ensure their survival, much like the Al Qaeda organization. The basic unit is a cell of five to ten members, including a leader, explosives experts, firearms manager, physical trainer and ideological counselor. Only the leader has contact with higher elements in the system, and members of different cells do not know each other. Above the cell is the subsector leader, followed by a zone leader who reports to the regional committee, which is below the National Central Committee, the ruling body. But Sendero alienated a large part of the population. Although it still operates, it appears that its time has past. Peru also has smaller terrorist groups such as Tupac Amaru, but they do not approach the scope of Sendero.

The 'Tri-border' area of South America where Argentina, Brazil and Paraguay meet is the central focus for Islamic extremism in Latin America. One group consistently tied to the region is Hezb'allah. The region has been used for fund-raising, as a hiding place, and to organize attacks on Israeli and U.S. Embassies in various South American capitals. Its popularity stems from difficult-to-enforce borders making it easy to flee from one country to the next as well as well-bribed officials in the area. Addressing the problems of this region will undoubtedly require more resources and more cooperation among the three countries.

TERRORISM IN ASIA

Although this book has already extensively discussed terrorism in Afghanistan and the repercussions it has for its neighbors, particularly Pakistan, it would be useful to examine briefly examples of terrorist activity in other Central, South, and East Asian states. The areas which deserve mention here are Kyrgyzstan, Tajikistan, Uzbekistan, Kashmir, Sri Lanka, Japan, the Philippines, Indonesia and North Korea.

In Central Asia, Kyrgyzstan, Tajikistan and Uzbekistan, to the north of Afghanistan and south of Russia, all face difficult challenges from international Islamic terrorism originating in Afghanistan. The group which causes the most problems for these three countries is the Islamic Movement of Uzbekistan (IMU). The IMU has declared a jihad against the governments of the three countries, hoping to destabilize and destroy those governments and install a fundamentalist Islamic

regime in their place. Afghanistan allows the IMU to operate from its soil, which greatly enhances their ability to launch terrorist attacks and subsequently escape. The IMU has terrorist camps in Afghanistan as well as in Tajikistan, although the bases in Tajikistan exist in spite of government opposition; the government has simply been unable to dislodge them.

IMU forces operate with relative impunity in the region, and their tactics generally involve mass hostage takings and terrorist bombings. In 1999, IMU terrorists entered Kyrgyzstan from Tajikistan and

created a ten week hostage crisis. They seized thirteen hostages, including four Japanese geologists, their interpreter, a general in the Kyrgyzstani Interior Ministry, and a number of Kyrgyzstani soldiers. Once the hostage-taking was successful, IMU forces poured in to support the hostage-takers, eventually numbering approximately 1,000. Their goal was to use the hostages to compel the Uzbek government to permit them to enter Uzbekistan, at which point they would try to overthrow the government. Uzbekistan denied their request, leaving the Kyrgyzstan military to address the problem. But the IMU militants defeated the Kyrgyzstan military in successive attempts to dislodge them from their mountain hiding places, and they eventually left only because after two months, the weather was turning cold. They eventually returned to one of their camps in Tajikistan on their own

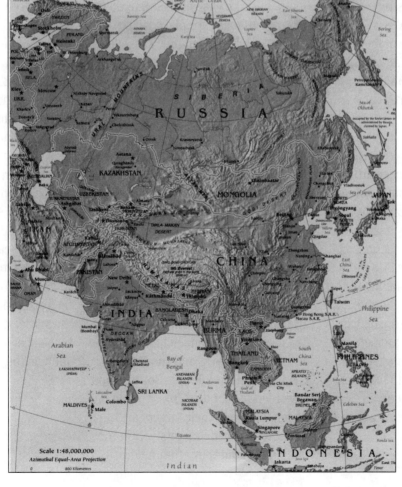

terms, and released all of the hostages with the exception of one soldier who had been murdered.

Earlier that same year, the IMU set off five car bombs simultaneously in downtown Tashkent, the capital of Uzbekistan, killing 16 and injuring 120. These attacks were aimed at assassinating Uzbek President Islom Karimov, but were unsuccessful. The government arrested and executed a number of suspects, but this did not appear to deter the group. The U.S. has removed some of its consular staff from the region, fearing for their safety. Uzbekistan has been successful with a few search-and-destroy missions against IMU strongholds, but it seems that without putting an end to Afghan assistance to the group, it will continue to execute large operations in the area.

In South Asia, Kashmir is a region which not only represents an intractable problem for its two contestants, India and Pakistan, but it also invites a wider scope of focus due to interest in the conflict among Muslims outside the region. Kashmir, in northern India and northeast Pakistan, is a region which both states claim as their territory, a subject which has been disputed for decades. In addition to the front-lines battles between Indian and Pakistani military forces, terrorist attacks have been launched against civilians deeper within the two countries' sections of this region. Some of these attacks have included horrible bombings of civilian trains, particularly in India, as well as hostage-takings. The Taliban has declared Kashmir an area of Islamic jihad, and has sent terrorists and soldiers to the region to participate in the battle against India on all fronts. It has also granted safe haven

to a number of Pakistani terrorists who are wanted by India for terrorist actions related to the Kashmir conflict, including a number of Air India hijackers. Pakistan has readily accepted the assistance of the Taliban in this regard, and also offers financial support to Kashmiri terrorist groups such as Harakat ul-Mujihadeen (HUM).

Just off the coast of India, in Sri Lanka, the separatist group Liberation Tigers of Tamil Eelam (LTTE) launches terrorist attacks such as suicide bombings as part of its campaign to win self-government for the Tamil people in the north of Sri Lanka. Their targets have ranged from the Sengalese ruling president, to moderate politicians representing their own ethnic background, and have also included civilian targets such as buses, trains, bus terminals, marketplaces and passenger ferry boats. Like the case of Kashmir, these terrorist attacks take place in the context of a larger military struggle, in this case, pitting the Tamil guerilla force against the Sri Lankan government army.

In East Asia, the Philippines experiences terrorism which is similar to the threat faced by Saudi Arabia. There is a heavy U.S. military presence in the Philippines which is the target of a number of terrorist organizations, including the Communist Party of the Philippines New People's Army. This group tends to ambush Philippine military and police forces, as well as U.S. military stations. The Philippines also contends with Islamic militants in its southern region, including groups such as Abu Sayyaf and the Moro Islamic Liberation Front. Both groups have received funding from Osama bin Laden, although their targets are primarily domestic targets within the Philippines and they often hold

hostages simply for ransom. Indonesia has also faced terrorism funded by Osama bin Laden, particularly as East Timor's secession made it appear possible to organize more revolutionary efforts in various parts of the country.

Japan has experienced terrorist troubles from the Aum Shinrikyo cult and from the Japanese Red Army group. 'Aum,' as it is sometimes known, is an anarchist group which famously perpetrated a deadly Sarin nerve gas attack on the Tokyo subway in March 1995. Japanese law enforcement officials have done an exemplary job of dismembering this cult, arresting many members and leaders and compelling compensation payments to the families of victims of the gas attack. The cult has openly pledged to discontinue its terrorist activities, although with the recent release from prison of an important leader, Fumihiro Joyu, it remains to be seen whether or not these activities will continue. The Japanese Red Army is an older anti-government group which has not been active recently, but whose members are hiding in Lebanon, Thailand and North Korea attempting to avoid extradition.

North Korea (The Democratic People's Republic of Korea) is East Asia's main state sponsor of terrorism. Although it does not act on the same scale as states such as Iran or Afghanistan, it is known for selling weapons directly and indirectly to terrorist groups in various parts of the world. It also provides safe haven to members of various terrorist groups such as the Japanese Red Army.

COMPARING AL QAEDA TO OTHER ORGANIZATIONS

From the preceding discussions of Osama bin Laden's Al Qaeda terrorist organization as well as other terrorist groups around the world, one important difference stands out: Al Qaeda has elements of a 'meta' terrorist organization which acts like a multinational holding company. But it also uses its own operatives to directly instigate terrorist attacks, and thus tends to operate on two levels.

On the meta-level, It locates promising terrorist groups which are deserving of funding, training and support, and it facilitates those groups' activities with money, weapons and guidance. It looks for organizations with similar guiding principles and ideologies. This type of sponsorship of other terrorist organizations flows from Al Qaeda's world headquarters in Afghanistan, and its CEO, Osama bin Laden.

Other terrorist organizations in the world tend to lack this level of support for other organizations, choosing to focus their efforts only on direct attacks in their own country or region. This is not true of all known terrorist organizations; some well-developed groups such as the GIA operate in more than one country, but such groups are already at least partially subsumed under the umbrella of the Al Qaeda organization.

Al Qaeda also is unique in the scale of its financing and the symbiotic relationship it has with its host country. Although many terrorist organizations derive funding from illegal means such as extortion and drug sales, particularly in Latin America, Al Qaeda is unmatched in its ability to combine legitimate enterprises around the world with a sprawling drug trade at home. When its members are sent abroad to start new cells, they open businesses and melt into the community while donating money back to the organization. In this way, cells can operate relatively independently, and are not wholly dependent on the central structure to supply them with financial necessities. In fact, they can actually supply the central structure with additional funds for its coffers. But in Afghanistan, Al Qaeda and Osama bin Laden have major stakes in the heroin and goods smuggling businesses. With millions of dollars in illegal proceeds each year, the group can immunize itself from international attempts to freeze bank accounts and otherwise prevent it from using assets it has collected. This illegal activity is tolerated in Afghanistan because it is advantageous to the ruling Taliban regime. The Taliban collects a 20% tax on drug sales, which forms the vast majority of its annual budget. Al Qaeda also helps the Taliban by providing soldiers and logistics to aid in its battles against rebel forces in the north. In this way, Al Qaeda occupies a unique position in the field of world terrorism by being one of the few groups to operate with the blessings and almost open encouragement of its government.

Otherwise, Al Qaeda operates like other terrorist organizations in the world, albeit on a larger scale. It has a global, rather than a regional vision, but is loosely organized enough that successful law enforcement work in one area does not provide many leads to continue searching elsewhere. To this end, it is structured similarly to the Sendero Luminoso movement in Peru, where members of one cell do not come into contact with or know members of other cells. Not lenient prosecution deals, not even torture could elicit the kind of useful information necessary to capture members of different cells as a result.

But some cells are so loosely connected to Al Qaeda as to be hardly a part of the network. This leads to the likelihood that, like organized crime and the mafia, other international terror networks are starting to form which operate mostly independently of Al Qaeda. This is suggested by the sheer numbers: of the 50,000 people who have trained in Afghan terrorist training camps in the past decade, only 10% have trained at Al Qaeda camps. If the Al Qaeda model of terrorism is proved successful, others will be encouraged to follow. Fighting this type of scourge will require a level of cooperation and vigilance among law enforcement and intelligence officials around the globe on a scale which has not yet been seen.

WHO'S WHO IN THE U.S. WAR ON TERRORISM?

GEORGE W. BUSH
U.S. President

President George W. Bush, as Commander-in-Chief, has ultimate authority for executing the 'war on terrorism' with military force, as well as through law enforcement efforts as the head of the Executive Branch of the U.S. Government. Although his background does not include extensive international experience, he has assembled a notable team of advisors with significant backgrounds in different aspects of international relations and law enforcement.

Bush was born in 1946, grew up in Midland, Texas, where his father worked in the oil business, and received his undergraduate degree from Yale in 1968. He described his post-college years as his 'nomadic' period, as he was relatively unfocused, working now and then as an agricultural management trainee and on various political campaigns. But he received an MBA from Harvard in 1975, returned to Texas to start an oil business, and married Laura Welch, a teacher and librarian, in 1977. He ran for the U.S. House of Representatives in 1978, but lost. In the 1980s, his oil business merged with another, which he later sold off for a significant profit. He gained inspiration from working on his father's presidential campaign in 1987 and 1988, then moved back to Texas and purchased the Texas Rangers baseball team with a group of investors.

He then surprised the State of Texas when he ran for and was elected governor in 1994. He was re-elected in 1998 and became the first Texas governor to be elected to two successive terms. He announced his candidacy for U.S. President in 1999, and eventually won the election in 2000 after a historic and unprecedented election where he lost the popular vote, but ended up winning after a five-week period of ballot re-counting in the pivotal State of Florida was ended by a surprising 5-4 Supreme Court vote.

DICK CHENEY
U.S. Vice President

Although the Vice President does not necessarily have a specified job in the event of a war or an extended campaign such as the war on terrorism, he is very close to the President and will likely play an important role in the formation of the administration's policy. His background, which includes time as Secretary of Defense, also lends himexperience with the types of issues that will be involved.

Cheney was born in 1941, grew up in Casper, Wyoming, and attended Yale for two years before dropping out. He married his high school sweetheart, Lynne, and later attended the University of Wyoming, where he received a bachelor's and a master's degree in political science in 1966. He went to Washington, D.C. to work for a congressman in 1969, where he was discovered by Rep. Donald Rumsfeld who was entering the administration of President Nixon. Cheney became Rumsfeld's special assistant, and followed him to his next job as White House counsel. In 1974, when President Ford selected Rumsfeld to be chief of staff, Cheney followed and became deputy chief of staff. One year later, when Rumsfeld became Secretary of Defense, Cheney became one of the youngest chiefs of staff in history.

Cheney returned to Wyoming in 1977, and was elected to the House of Representatives in 1979, where he remained until 1989. In 1989, President George Bush nominated him as Secretary of Defense, where he helped preside over the successful execution of the 1991 Gulf War. At the end of the Bush administration, he became CEO of the Halliburton oil drilling company in Dallas. He was selected as George W. Bush's running mate in July of 2000.

COLIN POWELL
U.S. Secretary of State

As Secretary of State, Colin Powell will play a crucial role in any war on terrorism. He will be primarily responsible for the diplomacy required to build an effective and broad coalition of states to contribute to military action, intelligence sharing, and law enforcement cooperation at the highest levels across the globe.

Powell was born in Harlem in 1937 to Jamaican immigrants and grew up in the South Bronx. He attended City College of New York, where he joined the ROTC Army program and graduated in 1958. He met his wife, Alma Vivian Johnson while stationed in Massachusetts in 1962, and was then sent to South Vietnam where he received a Purple Heart. On his second tour of duty, he received the Soldier's Medal for saving several men from a burning helicopter. He then read for a Master's degree in business administration at George Washington University, which he received in 1971, after which he worked as an analyst at the Pentagon. He then worked as an assistant to Caspar Weinberger and Frank Carlucci at the Office of Management and Budget, but returned to an Army assignment in South Korea as a battalion commander in 1973.

He served in several other assignments, including the 101st Airborne Division, a major general rank at the Pentagon, a Department of Energy advisor, and in 1983, military assistant to Secretary of Defense Caspar Weinberger. In 1986, he became Frank Carlucci's deputy at the National Security Council, and one year later, became Reagan's national security advisor. In 1989, under President Bush, he became the nation's youngest and first black chairman of the Joint Chiefs of Staff, the nation's highest military post. Here, along with Secretary of Defense Dick Cheney, he contributed greatly to the successful execution of Operation Desert Storm, and was awarded a congressional gold medal. He worked for charities at the end of the Bush administration, and became the Secretary of State under George W. Bush in January, 2001.

CONDOLEEZZA RICE
National Security Adviser

Condoleezza Rice is one of President Bush's most trusted advisors, and her position as national security adviser will offer her an opportunity to contribute her special experience with Russia and Eastern Europe. This will prove to be valuable experience given the importance of Russia in any coalition against terrorism.

Rice entered the University of Denver at age 15, graduating in political science at 19. She received a master's degree in political science from Notre Dame, and a doctoral degree in political science from the University of Denver. She taught arms control and disarmament at Stanford starting in 1981 where she became a professor. She spent a year as a fellow at the Hoover Institution,

and in 1986, went to work on nuclear strategic planning at the Joint Chiefs of Staff. She taught at Stanford for a few more years before returning to Washington, D.C. as director of Soviet and East European Affairs at the National Security Council in 1989 under President George Bush. During that time in Washington, she also served as special assistant to the President for national security affairs, and senior director for Soviet affairs at the National Security Council.

At the end of Bush's administration, she returned to Stanford where she eventually became university provost, after which she was selected as President George W. Bush's national security adviser.

DONALD RUMSFELD
Secretary of Defense

The Secretary of Defense will play a critical role in the planning and operation of any military component of an anti-terrorism war, and Donald Rumsfeld is one of the few individuals in history to hold that position in two different administrations.

Rumsfeld was born in Chicago in 1932, graduated from Princeton in 1954, and served as a Naval aviator until 1957. He worked for a congressman and then for an investment bank before being elected a U.S. Representative from Illinois in 1962. He held that position until resigning in 1969 to join the Nixon administration in a number of posts. In 1973, he served as the U.S. Ambassador to NATO in Brussels, and in 1974, he returned to serve as Chief of Staff to Gerald Ford. This was followed by his nomination as the youngest ever Secretary of Defense, a post he held from 1975 to 1977. In 1977, he received the nation's highest civilian award, the Presidential Medal of

Freedom. He went into private business afterwards, serving as the CEO of a number of corporations while simultaneously carrying out important government responsibilities including special envoy positions at treaty negotiations and Middle East peace negotiations and various advisory committee positions.

He remained in private business until he was nominated for the second time as Secretary of Defense by George W. Bush in 2001.

JOHN ASHCROFT
U.S. Attorney General

As U.S. Attorney General, John Ashcroft will be in charge of the law enforcement side of a war on terrorism, ranging from domestic criminal investigations to interacting with his counterparts on an international level in order to apprehend suspected terrorists.

Ashcroft was born and raised in Springfield, Missouri, and completed his undergraduate education at Yale, and his law school education at the University of Chicago, where he met his wife. At the age of 30, in 1972, he ran for a U.S. House of Representatives seat in Missouri, but lost in the Republican primary. But he was appointed Missouri state auditor in 1973, and was elected Missouri attorney general in 1976 and 1980. He won the governor's race in 1984, winning re-election in 1988. He became a U.S. Senator in 1994, where he continued to earn his reputation as one of the most conservative politicians in the U.S. When running for re-election in 2000, he lost to a deceased challenger, Mel

Carnahan, the Missouri governor who died three weeks before the election in a plane crash. His widow, Jean, was nominated to fill the seat.

Ashcroft was then nominated by President George W. Bush to become U.S. Attorney General in 2001.

TOM RIDGE
Director of the Office of Homeland Security

Although the details of the Office of Homeland Security are being worked out, it appears the office will attempt to coordinate the activities of the many different agencies in the federal government which have anti-terrorism responsibilities. This will likely be a difficult task, given the relative lack of cooperation between some of these agencies in the past. Nevertheless, it will require working closely with the Attorney General, FBI Director, CIA Director and other officials in order to develop consistent policies. Ridge grew up in public housing in Erie, Pennsylvania and received his undergraduate degree at Harvard. He won the Bronze Star in the Army in Vietnam, and received a law degree from Dickinson Law School. He then returned to Erie to practice law. He became an assistant district attorney for Erie County, and then won a narrow race for the House of Representatives. Ridge ran for governor of Pennsylvania in 1993 and was re-elected in 1998. In September 2001, he was named by George W. Bush to lead the newly-created Office for Homeland Defense.

ROBERT MUELLER
FBI Director

As director of the FBI, Mueller will work closely with Ashcroft and Ridge on all elements of the war on terrorism involving domestic criminal investigations.

Mueller was born in 1944, graduated from Princeton in 1966, and then received a master's degree in International Studies from NYU. He graduated from the University of Virginia law school in 1973. He served in the Marines for three years, including one year in Vietnam where he received the Bronze Star, two Navy Commendation Medals, a Purple Heart and the Vietnamese Cross of Gallantry. In the following years, he spent time as a prosecutor as well as a lawyer in private practice. He became an assistant to Attorney General Richard Thornburgh in the Department of Justice, and in 1986, became the U.S. Attorney for Massachusetts. In 1990, he was named Assistant Attorney General in the Criminal Division of the U.S. Department of Justice by President Bush, and in 1995, he became senior litigation counsel at the U.S. Attorney's Office for the District of Columbia. There, he became chief of the homicide section in 1997, and in 1998, he joined the U.S. Attorney's Office for the

Northern District of California, where he became U.S. Attorney in 1999. He was nominated Director of the FBI by President George W. Bush in July 2001.

GEORGE TENET
CIA Director

As CIA Director, George Tenet will play a crucial role in defending the U.S. against future terrorist attacks and capturing suspected terrorists. His agency is responsible for gathering intelligence information outside the borders of the U.S., which means not only cooperation with counterparts in various parts of the world, but collecting intelligence in difficult-to-penetrate regions of the world. He will also have to work with the Director of the FBI and the Office for Homeland Security to coordinate the activities of the agencies.

George Tenet received his undergraduate degree from Georgetown University, and a master's in international affairs from Columbia. He worked as a legislative assistant and legislative director for Senator John Heinz before joining the Senate Select Committee on Intelligence as a staff member. He became staff director of the Committee, and then served on President Clinton's national security transition team. He then became a special assistant to the President and senior director for intelligence programs at the National Security Council before becoming Deputy Director of Central Intelligence in 1995. He became Acting Director in 1996, and was sworn in as Director in July 1997.

THE U.S. ARMY

The US Army is the organization established by the United States to project its power by force or threat of force on land throughout the world.

THE COMBAT ARMS

Over the course of centuries, armies have evolved to reflect the basic means of projecting power, and so they divide their forces into three basic types: infantry, armor, and artillery. The infantry is the basic soldier: the man who carries the rifle or machinegun, who moves forward in the attack, or holds the line in the defense. Armor, which evolved from the cavalry, uses armored vehicles in the attack and the defense; importantly, the mobility of tanks is as vital as the armor itself. Finally artillery uses large scale guns (cannons, howitzers, also a form of cannon) and rocket launchers to attack the enemy at long ranges. The three combat arms receive support from a variety of additional units for supply, repair, transportation, and administration. But at the center of the US Army are the three combat arms.

ARMY UNITS

The army is a hierarchy, built on the principle of discipline and following orders. The basic army unit is the

Squad. An infantry squad consists of 6 to 12 men and is led by a sergeant. Both tank crews and artillery pieces are examples of squads.

A **platoon** is three to five (usually four) squads led by a lieutenant and a sergeant.

A **company** is three to five (usually four) platoons led by a captain. It is with great pride and tradition that the artillery calls its companies batteries and the armor identifies its companies as troops.

A **battalion** is three to five (usually four) companies led by a lieutenant colonel. Some U.S. tank units are called squadrons.

A **brigade** is three to six battalions and is led by a colonel or a brigadier general. Some U.S. tank units are called regiments.

A **division** is three to six brigades, plus other supporting battalions, and is led by a major general.

A **corps** (pronounced core) is three to six divisions and is commanded by lieutenant general. When several corps are grouped together, they are a field army (or just army) and commanded by a general.

Span of Control. The army believes in the concept of span of control: that a commander can best command between three and six subsequent, subordinant units. Thus, a lieutenant can best control between three and six squads; it is asking too much to expect him to control seven or ten, or twenty squads. Even the more experienced lieutenant colonel commanding a battalion (which has perhaps 64 squads) does not control them directly; he issues orders to the captains, who tell the lieutenants, who tell the squads.

Staff Officers. At battalion level and above, the commander has a staff which handles administration, intelligence, operations and training, and supply. At higher levels other staff functions are added such as civil affairs.

Numbers of troops. Press accounts of military forces do not usually mention unit designations; they do give round numbers as head counts.

Approximate Troop Counts

100 -	company
400 - 500	battalion
1000 - 2000	brigade
4000 - 12000	division

MAJOR WEAPONS

Infantry units are armed with the M16A1 rifle which can fire to about 300 meters. Armor units are armed with the M1A1 tank. This tank has a 50% chance of hitting a target tank at a range of 2000 meters (which is better than any other tank in the world). In all probability, tanks and armor units will not be deployed to mountainous regions of Afghanistan. Artillery units use a tank-like armored, self-propelled 155mm howitzer with a range of 18 km, and a lighter 155mm artillery piece which can be towed behind a truck.

The decision to deploy troops to Afghanistan (or to a base in a neighboring country) would be based on the capabilities of the units. The 10th Mountain Division seems an ideal choice based on its training for mountainous terrain. Light units (such as airborne divisions) are more likely to be deployed than heavy armored units.

U.S. Troop List

1st Armor Division
1st Infantry Division
3rd Infantry Division (Mech)
10th Mountain Division
101st Airborne Division
2nd Armored Cavalry Regiment

1st Cavalry Division
2nd Infantry Division
4th Infantry Division
5th Infantry Division
82nd Airborne Division
3rd Armored Cavalry Regiment

SPECIAL OPERATIONS FORCES

Congress in 1987 mandated the establishment of the U.S. Special Operations Command (USSOCOM,) which supplied funding and support to Army, Navy, and Air Force units dedicated to Special Operations and Low-Intensity Conflict (SO/LIC.) The U.S. Army's portion of these forces includes the Special Forces, the Rangers, Civil Affairs units, and Psychological Warfare units.

The Special Forces. The Special Forces first gained prominence in Vietnam as advisors to local troops and indiginous mountain tribes (the montanyards). The mission of Special Forces in that war was primarily training and directing military operations. After Vietnam, funding and support dropped to low levels, returning only after Congressional mandates. By the time of the Gulf War, Gen. H. Norman Schwarzkopf, described Special Forces as the "eyes and ears" of conventional forces and as the "glue that held coalition forces together." The Special Forces are organized into seven Groups, each with an assigned geographical region of interest. The Fifth Special Forces Group, stationed at Fort Campbell Kentucky, is assigned responsibility for South West Asia, which includes Afghanistan, and Northeast Africa.

SOAR. The Army's 160th Special Operations Aviation Regiment (Airborne) flies the helicopters for Army Special Operations and is equipped with MH-6 and AH-6 light helicopters, MH-60 helicopters and MH-47 heavy assault helicopters. The capabilities of the 160th SOAR (A) have been evolving since the early 1980s. Shortly after the failed hostage rescue mission, Desert One, in Iran, the Army formed this special aviation unit, drawing on the best aviators in the Army. Known as both Task Force 160 and the Night Stalkers because of its focus on night missions, it became the 160th Special Operations Aviation Regiment (Airborne) in 1990 and is assigned to the U.S. Army Special Operations Command.

The Rangers During the Vietnam era, the Army trained individual soldiers to be highly skilled, elite infantry men. These soldiers were called Rangers and they were assigned to positions in all divisions of the army. But In 1974, with the creation of the 1st and 2nd Ranger Battalions, the Rangers became an independant entity, charged with becoming the best light infantry in the world. By 1984, a third battalion and an improved command structure was established.

The Rangers are specially organized, equipped, and trained to rapidly deploy a credible military force to any region of the world. The Rangers are the premiere airfield seizure and raid unit in the Army. In order to remain proficient in all light infantry skills, Ranger units also focus on mission essential tasks that include movement to contact, ambush, reconnaissance, airborne and air assaults, and hasty defense.

The 75th Ranger Regiment, a headquarters for three battalions, is at Fort Benning, Georgia, as is the 3rd Battalion. The 1st Battalion is at Hunter Army Airfield, Georgia, and the 2nd Battalion is located at Fort Lewis, Washington.

Each battalion can deploy anywhere in the world with 18 hours notice.

Civil Affairs Civil affairs units work with civil authorities and civilian populations to lessen the impact of military operations on local populations.

Civil affairs specialists identify critical requirements needed by local citizens in war or disaster situations. They locate civil resources to support military operations, help minimize civilian interference with operations, support national assistance activities, plan and execute non-combatant evacuation, support counter-drug operations, and establish and maintain communications with civilian aid agencies and civilian commercial and private organizations.

In support of special operations, these culturally-oriented, linguistically-capable soldiers may also be tasked to provide functional expertise for foreign internal defense operations, unconventional warfare operations and direct action missions. The 96th Civil Affairs Battalion (Airborne) is the only active Army civil affairs unit. The remaining civil affairs forces are found in four Civil Affairs Commands, subordinate brigades and battalions in the Army Reserve.

PSYCHOLOGICAL WARFARE

Psychological Operations is the dissemination of truthful information to foreign audiences. It is intended to persuade rather than compel physically, and relies on logic, desire, and even fear, rather than force. The 4th Psychological Operations Group (Airborne) at Fort Bragg, North Carolina is the only active Army psychological operations unit. The 2nd and 7th Psychological Operations Groups are in the Army Reserve. Psychological Warfare units operate as "force multipliers;" they make traditional units more effective through their communications projects.

THE U.S. NAVY

The US Navy is the organization established by the United States to project its power with force or threat of force by sea throughout the world.

CARRIERS

It is often said that the central strength of the Navy is its aircraft carriers; in truth its central strength is its aircraft. Each aircraft carrier is the base for 70 to 80 aircraft, of which 24 are F-14A Tomcat fighters, 24 are F/A-18 Hornet fighter/attack planes, and 10 are A-6E Intruder long-range attack planes. The other aircraft based on the carrier have anti-submarine, electronic warfare, and early warning missions.

The Navy has nine active carriers on station around the world.

The Navy's Carriers
CV-63 Kitty Hawk
CV-64 Constellation
CV-67 John F. Kennedy
CVN-65 Enterprise
CVN-68 Nimitz
CVN-69 Dwight D. Eisenhower
CVN-70 Carl Vinson
CVN-71 Theodore Roosevelt
CVN-72 Abraham Lincoln
CVN-73 George Washington
CVN-74 John C. Stennis
CVN-75 Harry Truman

CV indicates an aircraft carrier. CVN indicates a nuclear powered aircraft carrier.

The carriers are almost defenseless by themselves. Their hulls are not especially well-armored. They have some close range defenses against missiles and aircraft, but the effectiveness of their defenses is not enough to guarantee stopping an attack. Instead, each carrier is the center of a task force of other ships whose function it is to keep any potentially threatening ships away from the carrier. At the same time, the carrier's radars monitor the skies for enemy air threats, and the carrier's aircraft flies protection which is called combat air patrol to head off potential air attacks.

. SEA LAUNCHED CRUISE MISSILE
BGM-109 *TOMAHAWK*

TOP VIEW

SIDE VIEW

CRUISE MISSILES

The Navy can also project its power through its Tomahawk cruise missiles. The Tomahawk is a long-range missile powered by a jet engine; this power source gives the missile a long range in a relatively small package. It can be launched from either surface ships such as cruisers or destroyers or from submarines. Flying at 550 miles per hour, the Tomahawk has a range of about 1,000 miles, delivering a 1,000 lb warhead of high explosive or cluster bombs which are a kind of lethal fragmentary grenade. The guidance system for the cruise missile uses high resolution satellite maps and can fly the Tomahawk through a 30 foot window anywhere in the world; the GPS (Global Positioning System) upgrade is supposed to reduce this window to slightly more than 3 feet. The problems inherent with the cruise missile are three-fold: first, it must have a target, and second, in most situations the missile takes between one and two hours to reach the target, and third, there are some potential targets which are beyond the 1,000 mile range from sea based ships. In its latest procurement version, the Tomahawk cost about $600,000 each. The Tomahawk can be fitted with a 250 kiloton nuclear warhead.

SPECIAL OPERATIONS FORCES

When Congress created the U.S. Special Operations Command (USSOCOM), the Navy's contribution was the SEALS and a special counter-terrorism section of the SEALS called Naval Special Warfare Development Group (NSWDG) or DEVGRU.

The SEALs Sea-Air-Land (SEAL) Teams began as Underwater Demolition Teams clearing beaches chosen for amphibious landings in World War II and Korea. In January 1962, the first SEAL Teams were commissioned to conduct unconventional warfare, counter-guerilla warfare, and clandestine operations in maritime and riverine environments in Vietnam. After the Vietnam War, the SEAL program expanded to include SEALs, SEAL Delivery Vehicle Teams, and Special Boat Units. There are six SEAL Teams operating: SEAL Teams 1, 3, and 5 at Coronado Naval Base, San Diego, California, and SEAL teams 2, 4, and 8 at Little Creek, Virginia.

DEVGRU After the failed 1980 attempt to rescue American hostages at the Iranian Embassy (Operation Eagle Claw), Seal Team 6 was created and is responsible for counter terrorist operations in a maritime environment. The SEALs had already begun counter-terrorist training and were judged mission-ready by early 1981. Currently called the Naval Special Warfare Development Group (NSWDG) and based in Dam Neck Virginia, this unit is under the direct command of NAVSPECWARGRU, however it is also a component of Joint Special Operations Command (JSOC - Pope AFB, North Carolina), along with other counter terrorism units such as Delta Force and the 160th Special Operations Aviation Regiment (SOAR). Some reports say that DEVGRU is authorized to conduct preemptive actions against terrorists and terrorist installations. DEVGRU maintains its own helicopter support unit (2 squadrons with 18 HH-60H for SEAL transport and support), but trains with the Army's 160th SOAR. It is estimated the group has 200 operational troops.

Aircraft Carrier, Nimitz Class, USS Eisenhower

Nimitz Class Air Craft Carrier

Length, overall: 1,092 feet Flight Deck Width: 252 feet
Beam (width): 134 feet
Displacement: Approx. 97,000 tons full load

Speed: 30+ knots (34.5+ miles per hour)
Aircraft: 85
Cost: about $4.5 billion each
Power Plant: Two nuclear reactors, four shafts

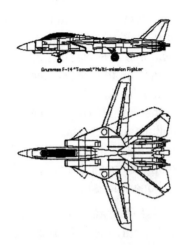

Grumman F-14 "Tomcat" Multi-mission Fighter

The Grumman F-14 Tomcat is a supersonic, twin-engine, variable sweep wing, two-place strike fighter. The Tomcat's primary missions are air superiority, fleet air defense and precision strikes against ground targets.
Function: Carrier-based multi-role strike fighter
Unit Cost: $38 million
Length: 61 feet 9 inches
Height: 16 feet
Wingspan: 64 feet unswept, 38 feet (swept
Ceiling: Above 50,000 feet
Speed: Super Sonic (Mach 2+)
Crew: Two (pilot and radar officer)
Armament: Up to 13,000 pounds to include AIM-54 Phoenix missile, AIM-7 Sparrow missile, AIM-9 Sidewinder missile, air-to-ground precision strike ordnance, and one M61A1/A2 Vulcan 20mm cannon.

F/A-18 Hornet

Description: All-weather fighter and attack aircraft. The single-seat F/A-18 Hornet is the nation's first strike-fighter. It was designed for traditional strike applications such as interdiction of enemy movement and close air support without compromising its fighter capabilities.
Length: 56 feet
Height: 15 feet 4 inches
Wingspan: 40 feet 5 inches
Ceiling: 50,000+ feet
Speed: Super Sonic (Mach 1.7+)
A,C and E models: One
B,D and F models: Two
Armament: One M61A1/A2 Vulcan 20mm cannon;

External payload: AIM 9 Sidewinder, AIM 7 Sparrow, AIM-120 AMRAAM, Harpoon, HARM, SLAM, SLAM-ER, Maverick missiles; Joint Stand-Off Weapon (JSOW); Joint Direct Attack Munition (JDAM); various general purpose bombs, mines and rockets.

THE U.S. AIR FORCE

The U.S. Air Force is the organization established by the United States to project its power by force or threat of force, worldwide through the use of airpower. There are three basic missions assigned to the air force: to achieve air superiority in any contested area of the globe, to conduct aerial bombardment operations in hostile situations, and to provide air transport to the US military.

Air Superiority. The Air Force believes that it must control its airspace in order to maximize its efficiency and to protect those it is supporting. The entire purpose of its fighter aircraft is to dominatethe aircraft of its enemy. The Air Force has in its inventory F-15 and F-16 fighter aircraft for this purpose.

Aerial Bombardment. The core of this Air Force mission is Global Attack: the ability to conduct aerial bombardment anywhere in the world. The Air Force strategic bombardment mission has always included a global reach, but in recent history improved guidance of munitions (such as laser guided bombs) has increased the need and the ability to bomb very well-defined locations. The Air Force uses B52, B1, and B2 bombers for this purpose.

Air Transport. The Air Force provides the transport aircraft which airlifts US troops and equipment anywhere in the world. This strategic airlift capability makes use of C-130, C-5, and C-17 aircraft.

SPECIAL OPERATIONS

The Air Force component of USSO-COM is the Air Force Special Operations Command, headquartered at Hurlburt Field, Florida. The initial reserve call-ups of September 22, 2001 included 56 individual reserve mobilizations for AFSOC. AFSOC flies AC-130 gunships, MC-130 transport and refuelling aircraft, and MH-53 helicopters (the M indicates aircraft and helicopters specially configured for special operations).

16th Special Operations Wing is based at Hurlburt Field, Florida.

352nd Special Operations Group is based at RAF Mildenhall, England and is responsible for missions in Europe.

353rd Special Operations Group is based at Kadena Air Base, Japan, and is responsible for missions in the Pacific.

720th Special Tactics Group (Hurlburt Field) is tasked to provide air traffic control for air assaults, close air support, gunship missions, and tactical weather forecasting for Special Operations.

B-1 Long-Range, multi-role, heavy bomber
Length: 146 feet
Wingspan: 137 feet extended forward, 79 feet swept aft
Height: 34 feet
Weight: Empty, approximately 190,000 pounds
Speed: 900-plus mph (supersonic)
Range: Intercontinental, unrefueled
Ceiling: More than 30,000 feet
Crew: Four (aircraft commander, copilot, offensive systems officer and defensive systems officer)

Armament: Three internal weapons bays can accommodate up to 84 Mk-82 general purpose bombs or Mk-62 naval mines, 30 CUB-87/89 cluster munitions or CBU-97 Sensor Fused Weapons and up to 24 GBU-31 JDAM GPS guided bombs or Mk-84 general purpose bombs
Date Deployed: June 1985
Unit Cost: $200-plus million per aircraft
Inventory: 51 primary mission aircraft inventory

B-2 Multi-Role Heavy Bomber
Length: 69 feet
Height: 17 feet
Wingspan: 172 feet
Speed: High subsonic
Ceiling: 50,000 feet
Takeoff Weight (Typical): 336,500 pounds
Range: Intercontinental, unrefueled
Armament: Conventional or nuclear weapons
Payload: 40,000 pounds
Crew: Two pilots
Unit cost: $1.3 billion
Date Deployed: December 1993
Inventory: Active force: 21

B-52 Heavy Bomber
Length: 159 feet, 4 inches
Height: 40 feet, 8 inches
Wingspan: 185 feet
Speed: 650 miles per hour
Ceiling: 50,000 feet
Weight: Approximately 185,000 pounds empty
Maximum Takeoff Weight: 488,000 pounds
Range: Unrefueled 8,800 miles
Armament: Approximately 70,000 pounds mixed ordnance -- bombs,

mines and missiles. (Modified to carry air-launched cruise missiles, Harpoon anti-ship and Have Nap missiles.)
Crew: Five
Accommodations: Six ejection seats
Unit Cost: $74 million

Date Deployed: February 1955
Inventory: 85 plus 9 reserve

C-130 Tactical and Intratheater Airlift
Length: 97 feet, 9 inches
Height: 38 feet, 3 inches
Wingspan: 132 feet, 7 inches
Speed: C-130E: 345 mph
Ceiling: 33,000 feet with 45,000 pounds payload
Payload (C-130E): maximum 20 tons for 1800 miles; normal 16 tons. 6 pallets or 92 combat troops or 64 paratroopers.
Unit Cost: C-130E, $11.9 million
Inventory: Active force, 186 active; 217 Air National Guard; 107 Air Force Reserve.

C-141 Cargo and Troop Transport
Wingspan: 160 feet
Length: 168 feet, 4 inches
Height: 39 feet, 3 inches
Speed: 500 mph
Ceiling: 41,000 feet at cruising speed
Range: Unlimited with in-flight refueling
Load: 200 troops, 155 paratroops, 103 litters and 14 seats, or 31 tons.
Unit Cost: $42.3 million (FY98 dollars)
Crew: Five or six
Inventory: 74 Active duty; 28 Air National Guard; 68 Air Force Reserve

B-1

B-2

C-17 Cargo and Troop Transport
Wingspan: 169 feet 10 inches (to winglet tips)
Length: 174 feet
Height: 55 feet 1 inch
Speed: 450 mph
Range: Global with in-flight refueling
Crew: Three (two pilots and one loadmaster)
Load: 102 troops/paratroops or 77 tons.
Unit Cost: $236.7 million (FY98 dollars)
Inventory: 58 Active duty; 6 Air National Guard.

C-5 Outsize Cargo Transport
Wingspan: 222.9 feet
Length: 247.1 feet
Height: 65.1 feet
Maximum Cargo: 122 tons
Speed: 518 mph
Range: 6,320 nautical miles (empty)

C-130

C-17

C-5

F-15

F-16

B-52

Crew: 7 (pilot, co-pilot, two flight engineers and three loadmasters)
Unit Cost: C-5B - $179 million (FY98 dollars)

F-15E Strike Eagle Air-to-ground attack aircraft
Wingspan: 42.8 feet
Length: 63.8 feet
Height: 18.5 feet
Speed: Supersonic (Mach 2.5)
Range: 2,400 miles ferry range with conformal fuel tanks and three external fuel tanks
Armament: One 20mm multibarrel gun mounted internally with 500 rounds of ammunition. Four AIM-7F/M Sparrow missiles and four AIM-9L/M Sidewinder missiles, or eight AIM-120 AMRAAM missiles. Any air-to-surface weapon in the Air Force inventory (nuclear and conventional)
Crew: Pilot and weapon officer
Unit cost: $31.1 million
Inventory: 217 Active force.

F-16 Multirole Fighter
Length: 49 feet, 5 inches
Height: 16 feet
Wingspan: 32 feet, 8 inches
Speed: 1,500 mph
Ceiling: Above 50,000 feet
Range: More than 2,000 miles ferry range
Armament: One M-61A1 20mm multi-barrel cannon with 500 rounds; external stations can carry up to six air-to-air missiles, conventional air-to-air and air-to-surface munitions and electronic countermeasure pods
Unit cost: $30.1 million
Crew: F-16C, one; F-16D, one or two.

CONVENTIONAL DEPLOYMENT

The military creates its plans for future wars long before they ever start. Traditionally, armed forces planners have used the lessons of the most recent war to create plans and strategies that will refight that war more effectively. That planning serves a deterrent purpose...it makes a re-fighting of the most recent war less likely. But even the military recognizes that the next war may not be like the last one, and that good plans must cover many different contingencies.

Contingencies, however, are alternatives to the basic plan, and the basic structure of American military plans is not a secret; its very existence is intended to be a deterrent. It is possible to examine America's war plans and evaluate how they will be implemented in a war against terrorism. Strategic American war planning is based on three principles:

Two Wars At Once. The size of the American military is based on the assumption that it must be able to fight two major wars at once. If it were not so structured, the United States could find itself engaged with one enemy in a major conflict and vulnerable to an attack by another enemy. During the Vietnam War, even with 500,000 troops committed to Southeast Asia, the U.S. maintained credible forces in Europe (and Korea) to deter and, if necessary, respond to other potential threats. For broad

planning purposes, the planners assume that the two wars will be with North Korea (or somewhere in the Far East) and Iraq (or somewhere in the Middle East).

A War Has Four Phases. Most plans for conventional war assume that it will proceed through four distinct but perhaps overlapping phases:

4 PHASES OF A WAR

HALTING THE INVASION

FORCE BUILDUP

COUNTEROFFENSIVE

POSTWAR STABILITY

American plans assume reaction to aggression (Halting The Invasion) rather than a war of aggression in which case the phase would be Invasion. The Gulf War is a classic example of the four phases. U.S. and allied forces moved to halt the invasion by deploying forces to Saudi Arabia and then built up forces, along with their support units, in the region. Ultimately, those forces were brought into action with specific goals. Once achieved, most forces are removed while some remain to administer the post-war requirements of repatriation and peace enforcement.

This four phase structure for a war is rudimentary, but it is also applicable to any type of conflict. No matter whether the conflict is going to be a conventional land-based war, a guerilla war, a bombing campaign, or a

series of special operations raids, it will inevitably proceed through these four phases.

Positive Climate. Every war is fought in a variety of environments: political, diplomatic, economic, even moral, and its eventual resolution depends on each of those environments being positive. The Gulf War and its aftermath reflects the importance of such positive environments: the Coalition which brought together the many different nations of the Middle East and Europe against Iraq, reflects the need for, and achievement of, a positive diplomatic environment. At the same time, the limitations of the environment meant that once Kuwait was liberated, there was not sufficient international support for further military efforts to topple Saddam Hussein's government. The diplomatic environment shifted from positive to neutral, and was enough to end further millitary efforts.

WHAT'S NEEDED

To wage a war, the U.S. needs forces in place and bases to support them.

Conventional Forces. U.S. military planners believe that the force required for a War, (they call it a Major Regional Conflict) in a conventional sense, includes five Army divisions, five Marine brigade-equivalents, and, over the long term, continuing reinforcement by Army National Guard brigades. Air Force planners believe they need 10 Fighter Wings (of about 72 aircraft each) and 100 long-range bombers. Navy planners expect to deploy a fleet of four or five aircraft carriers each with 70 to 80 planes, of which 50 can fight and 25 can bomb, plus one or two Marine Corp Air Wing (about 75 planes.)

Bases. Modern armies require bases on the ground to provide the supply and maintenance so necessary to the tools of modern warfare; rarely do military units spend long periods of time out in the countryside fighting or even patrolling. Modern air forces require air bases within reasonable range of the combat zone; while aerial refuelling gives aircraft a virtually unlimited range, it is unreasonable to expect pilots or aircraft to routinely fly great distances and aerial refuel multiple times. Modern naval forces are effectively able to remain on station for months at a time, but even they require ports at which they can refuel, replenish, and rearm.

HOW SOON?

Historically, the first units in Desert Storm arrived in Saudi Arabia on August 8, 1990, six days after the invasion of Kuwait; the first major troop units arrived in Saudi Arabia (by sea) on August 28, less than a month after the invasion. The first battle by U.S. forces in the ground war took place January 29, 1991, 180 days after the invasion of Kuwait.

The Army has a long term goal of placing a battle-ready brigade anywhere in the world in 4 days, a division in place in 5 days, and five divisions in place in a month. Their current capability is closer to a brigade in 4 days, a division in 12 days, and 5 divisions in three months.

The Marines expect to put a Marine Expeditionary Force on the ground within two weeks.

The Air Force can move aircraft to established bases in a matter of days.

Traditional warfare envisions air forces bombing enemy installations, naval forces patrolling the sea, and ground forces attacking and seizing territory.

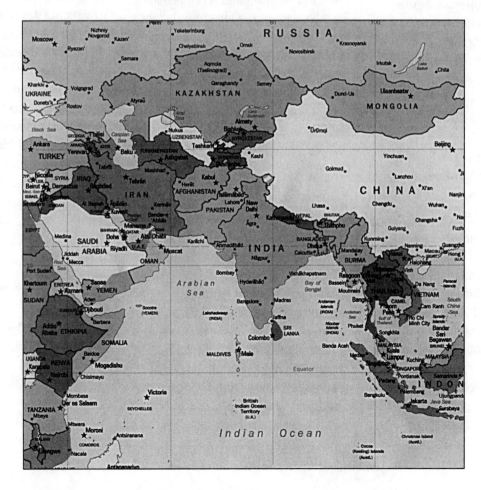

FOUR GOALS FOR THE FIRST STRIKE

The first strike of the War Against Terrorism is important because it creates world public opinion about military operations and their effectiveness. It must be a victory, but it also must achieve that victory in a way that does not attack the non-combatant public, advances the purpose of destroying terrorists, and rallies public support. There are four supportable goals that fit this criteria.

1 To achieve air supremacy by eliminating the ability of the Taliban government to conduct air operations against the Coalition. This includes the operations of radars and air defenses. A collateral effect is to strengthen the Northern Alliance by weakening the Taliban.

2 To create maximum damage to the Al Qaeda infrastructure, including killing its members and destroying its facilities. There is strong support in the Coalition for eliminating Osama bin-Laden and destroying Al Queda.

3 To cripple the finances of the Taliban government by destroying their drug manufacturing facilities and their stockpiles of opium. Public opinion is behind destroying drugs at their source; eliminating stocks of drugs reduces drug abuse problems in Europe, Asia, and America. Elimination of drug stocks drastically reduces a major source of funding for the Taliban, Al Qaeda, and other terrorist groups in Central Asia.

4 To enable the provision of humanitarian relief to the people of Afghanistan. The past year's drought and the continuing war have created massive suffering in the country. The concept of humanitarian relief, already supported by the Coalition, relieves suffering and creates positive perceptions.

ONE POSSIBLE SCENARIO

• Prior to operations, diplomatic initiatives create a favorable Coalition environment. Permissions for advanced bases for ground troops and aircraft are negotiated in Kazakhstan and Uzbekistan.

• Major air lifts position USAF strike aircraft at airfields in Kazakhstan. Simultaneously, special operations support aircraft are positioned in remote airfields in Kazakhstan and Uzbekistan.

• Special operations forces are prepositioned in Central Asia, briefed for their specific missions, and undergo intense rehearsal and training.

• Intelligence gathering details precise potential target locations throughout Afghanistan. Targets are monitored for changes over time, and evaluated for suitability, including availability and potential for collateral damage.

• Weather forecasters analyze climate and weather conditions and set a window of opportunity for a major operation.

• The final date is set (perhaps on less than six hours notice) and the order is given.

• Cruise missile launches from the Gulf of Arabia hit major military targets in Afghanistan. Strike aircraft attack airfields, air bases, fuel supplies, and radar sites. Selected targets are within reach and are hit to clear the way for Northern Alliance advances.

• Special operations forces launch and simultaneously strike throughout Afghanistan.

• Terrorist camps are raided and terrorists are eliminated. Military armaments are destroyed in place. Selected materials are captured and removed for intelligence purposes and perhaps for evidence or demonstrations of proof in dealing with the Coalition. In selected areas, video images are made for examination by intelligence and higher level commanders (and for potential release to the media).

• Drug stockpiles and drug production laboratories are raided, photographed and videotaped, and destroyed in place.

• Raid locations are hit by strike aircraft as the special operations forces withdraw.

• Northern Alliance forces, aware of the first strike operations only after they have begun, begin an offensive to expand their controlled territory.

• U.S. light infantry forces (probably Rangers) seize a major air base in northern Afghanistan (Mazar-e Sharif) to create an airhead. An overland route is cleared to the border with Uzbekistan.

• Immediately after the airhead is established and secured, the Rangers are detailed to provide security and are reinforced with heavier forces, perhaps units from the 6th Mountain division, including light armor and air defenses.

• The airhead becomes a hub for the shipment of humanitarian relief, administered jointly by Saudi (and

other) funded Islamic Relief agencies and the United States. U.S. Army Civil Affairs forces supervise relief efforts while assisting in the establishment of local government. Psychological Warfare forces (perhaps using another name) convey positive connotations to the relief effort to the local population.

• First Strike hostilities end within 48 hours. Humanitarian relief is in place within five days. At a minimum, the humanitarian relief operation is billed as the primary purpose of the operation. Each additional success is claimed, and any failures are dismissed as merely ancillary.

• The Strike ends in time to allow preparations for winter, and relief forces are in place to assist in recovery and crop planting in the spring.

WILL AFGHANISTAN BECOME ANOTHER VIETNAM?

THE VIETNAM WAR

Vietnam is a tropical country of about 127,000 square miles (slightly larger than New Mexico.) In 1965 Vietnam had a population of about 75 million people. South Vietnam was half that size in area and population.

The Vietnam War (1964-1975) pitted Communist North Vietnam, supported logistically by the Soviet Union, against nominally democratic South Vietnam, supported by the United States and many South East Asian nations. The common view was that the western democracies needed to stand up to Communist expansion or each South East Asian nation would, in turn, fall to encroaching Communism (this was the "domino theory.") The North Vietnamese strategy was to wage a guerilla war, with the help of local resistance fighters called the Viet Cong, throughout the South. Adjacent Laos and Cambodia supplied the Viet Cong with weapons and munitions. U.S . involvement came initially in the form of military aid and military advisors. What began with about 700 advisors in 1964 rose to a peak of 543,000 conventional military troops in 1968. A divided public in the U.S., combined with high U.S. casualty levels, made continuing participation in the war increasingly difficult, and the U.S. withdrew in March of 1975.

THE AFGHAN WAR

Afghanistan is a mountainous country of about 251,000 square miles (slightly less than Texas) and in 2001 about 26 million in population.

The Soviet Afghan War (1979-1989) was fought between the Soviet Union and Afghanistan. Years of diplomatic and covert political influence were dedicated to transforming the government of Afghanistan into a Communist state; this effort culminated in a series of coups in 1978 and 1979, and a Soviet invasion in late 1979. Although the Soviets originally planned to withdraw their military after several months, they stayed for ten years. They were faced with a fanatic Afghan resistance fighting an unconventional war in forbidding terrain, something they were not trained or equipped to do. Involvement in Afghanistan was downplayed and sometimes ignored by the Soviet press, and casualties were reported at far lower levels than actually occurred. By 1989 the drain on morale within the army, and in the general population made the war an

unacceptable commitment, and the Soviets withdrew.

THE WAR ON TERRORISM

The War on Terrorism was fought between the U.S. led-Coalition and Moslem heretic terrorists in Afghanistan.

Following the terrorist attacks on the World Trade Center and the Pentagon, the U.S. forged a strong coalition of nations to suppress established terrorist bases in Afghanistan and elsewhere. Traditional military operations were restricted to air and cruise missile attacks on carefully targeted bases. Diplomatic maneuvers isolated the Taliban government as the Northern Alliance gained legitimacy. With the overhanging threat of Coalition bombing preventing Taliban counter-attacks, the Northern Alliance gradually increased its territory within the country. Special Operations Forces reduced or eliminated the ability of terrorists to function. More importantly, massive humanitarian aid programs to Afghan refugees in Pakistan and in Northern Alliance territory improved dismal living conditions; Civil Affairs programs rebuilt infrastructure, reestablished government at the local level, and developed economic alternatives to the opium trade. By the end of 2003, the Afghan portion of the terrorist network was impotent and unable to function.

WEAPONS OF MASS DESTRUCTION

For some time, experts have been concerned about the potential use of weapons of mass destruction (WMD,) and the term has acquired a variety of definitions. The traditional military definition of WMD is nuclear, chemical, or biological weapons which, by their nature cause mass casualties and extensive property damage. Traditional military weaponry such as explosive artillery shells, aerial bombs, machine gun fire and land mines lie outside the definition. In anticipation of possible terrorist use, however, the technical definition in U.S. law includes large explosive devices such as car bombs. The FBI states that a weapon becomes a WMD when the consequences of its release overwhelm local responders. California law includes the intentional release of industrial chemicals or agents as a weapon. Under such definitions, the term WMD applies to the bombing of the Alfred P. Murrah Federal Building in Oklahoma City, Oklahoma in 1995. Similarly, the term clearly applies to the attacks on the World Trade Center and the Pentagon.

CHEMICAL WEAPONS

Modern society is filled with routine shipments of chemicals for industry and agriculture. Hazardous material data sheets accompany these chemicals detailing their various dangerous characteristics. Long before these modern safety measures were implemented, the military looked at dangerous chemicals and considered how to use them against the enemy.

TRADITIONAL CHEMICAL WEAPONS

Modern chemical warfare began in World War I with the introduction of Chlorine, Mustard Gas, and Phosgene to the trench warfare battlefields of France and Russia. Their consideration was forced by the trench warfare stalemates of 1915, and they were introduced with little advance planning or research. Reaction to their use produced a ban on chemical weapons under international law, but that did not stop research into new types of chemical weapons, including nerve gases which are quickly absorbed and block nerve impulses, resulting in convulsions, respiratory paralysis, and death.

Most chemical weapons can be created in a makeshift laboratory in small quantities in much the same way that similar makeshift laboratories are used to make methamphetamine from decongestant and various household chemicals. For example, truly sophisticated terrorists might synthesize the relatively harmless precursors to VX nerve gas by utilizing 2 fairly simple chemicals.

CHEAP CHEMICAL WEAPONS

The most probable threat from terrorists, however, is not synthesized cutting edge nerve gases; it would be far easier for a terrorist to acquire an industrial gas such as chlorine, or an industrial chemical such as phosgene, in a carload quantity and arrange its release in either a select, targeted outdoor setting or a confined indoor setting.

Most calculations of chemical weapons effectiveness address an exact killing dose ("a pinhead of liquid on the skin kills instantly!") Distributing chemical weapons is a very inexact procedure. Though the notion that just a pinhead sized dose of a chemical agent could kill a person, it is probably beyond the means of a terrorist or even a military delivery system, to accurately divide and distribute such an agent with significant results.

NUCLEAR WEAPONS

Even the smallest nuclear weapon represents a massive explosive potential. A 20 kiloton bomb at the site of the World Trade Center would have had lethal blast effects reaching to the Hudson River to the west and the East River to the east. In addition, it would create massive fires. The Hiroshima and Nagasaki bombs of World War II were air bursts; a nuclear explosion on the ground would create massive amounts of long term nuclear contamination.

One criticism of proposed new U.S. missile defenses is that they do not affect or deter the suitcase bomb (or more specifically, the suitcase nuke) which can be smuggled into  the U.S. with relative ease. That suitcase sized atomic bomb represents a small, but increasingly more likely, nuclear threat. While the original World War II atomic bombs weighed 5 tons each and had a yield of about 13 kilotons of TNT, U.S. Weapons technology in the 1960's created the Davy Crockett warhead; it weighed just 51 pounds and had a yield of 20 tons of TNT (about eight times more powerful than the Oklahoma City truck bomb.)

EXISTING NUCLEAR WEAPONS

The challenge of creating a nuclear weapon is threefold: obtaining the detailed specifications and plans for manufacturing the device, obtaining the appropriate nuclear material (and machining it to the proper specifications,) and creating the other components of the bomb. Such an undertaking is probably only within the capacity of nation states. Much more likely, a terrorist organization would acquire a nuclear weapon through some fortuitous opportunity such as a clandestine theft from poorly guarded stockpiles.

THE CHEAP ALTERNATIVE

A much easier route to a nuclear weapon is to forego the explosion and proceed directly to the radiation effects. Simply scattering nuclear material as dust would contaminate territory, making it unusable to its inhabitants or anyone else for years, perhaps centuries, to come. Such an attack could be made even more catastrophic if left undetected. Allowing a gradual realization of the effects increases the fear factor; if coupled with a target area which already has nuclear power facilities, the true cause might never come out.

BIOLOGICAL WEAPONS

People have feared plague and disease for centuries. This fear of sickness creates panic and is, to the terrorist, an ideal vehicle for a terrorist campaign. Even a nation which never intends to deploy biological warfare against an enemy needs to conduct related research, if only to develop defenses for them. Three of the diseases commonly mentioned are plague, anthrax, and smallpox.

THE PLAGUE

Bubonic Plague (the Black Death) devastated Europe in the 13th Century, killing one out of three people over the course of ten years. Bubonic Plague is spread by fleas on rats. Modern sanitation makes it unlikely that rats can be employed for an effective attack. The related Pneumonic Plague is spread by aerial particles exhaled by its sufferers. Modern public health measures make it unlikely that it could gain a large foothold in society.

SMALLPOX

Smallpox was actually common in the United States early in the 20th Century, but a  strong medical campaign has eliminated it as a disease; samples remain on file in secure labs in the U.S. and Russia. It is improbable that it would be stolen and then released.

ANTHRAX

The use of anthrax as a weapon has been researched by governments since 1915. During World War II, though anthrax was not used, a number of weapon delivery systems were developed and during the Cold War, the accidental release of anthrax from a research facility resulted in the death of 66 of the 77 diagnosed cases. Because anthrax is fairly simple to produce, its use by terrorists is of substantial concern. Additionally, its persistence in contaminating soil can result in significant residual affects. Gruinard Island, where the British conducted anthrax experiments has been banned from human entry for over fifty years.

THE CHEAP ALTERNATIVE

Hospitals deal with diseases on a daily basis. The routine medical environment is an easy source for medically trained terrorists to find one or more virulent diseases. After harvesting two (or even three) such common diseases, carefully selected for their infectiousness and their ability to survive as aerosols in the air, the terrorist could incubate it to create large quantities of this infectious soup and distribute it. One method of distribution that has generated widespread concern is the use of a crop duster. Though it is possible that a crop duster could dump such a contagen on a city, studies in Chicago, using innocuous particles, indicated that heat generated from city infrastructure would create an upward draft, that in the case of Chicago, would distribute none of the intended contagin to victims below. Alternative and potentially more deadly methods of distribution may target confined public areas by way of an air-conditioning system or a subway. Public water systems are treated against infection and are poor means of distributing diseases. No disease is likely to infect people beyond a limited geographic area, or even every person in a small area. Even hospital populations subject to accidental exposures have not shown large infection rates.

CYBER WEAPONS

When a random virus disables the average user's computer, or computer attacks disable web sites or e-vendors, users are inconvenienced. Because there aren't enough protections in place and because it is difficult to control individual users and even large companies, the Nation's vast network of vital computer systems is vulnerable.

HACKING

The miracle of the modern computer network is that it allows remote operation of many of modern society's mechanisms: the electric grid, the gas supply system, or the air traffic control system.
Although prudent programmers put into place a variety of safeguards to prevent hacking, it is conceivable for cyber-terrorists working thousands of miles away to break into vital systems using hacking applications, or simple stolen passwords. Remotely controlled changes in gas pressure in supply lines could produce explosions in many of the homes and businesses served by the line. Electric power could be interrupted. The minimum effect is inconvenience; the potential maximum effect is large scale loss of life.

VIRUSES

Modern viruses are nuisances and represent a threat to individual computers. Viruses and anti-viruses evolve in a continuing interaction. The next generation of virus, however, will be a change, not in structure but in purpose. Joined with the virus will be detectors searching for specific programs (life support system controllers in hospitals; traffic control systems; or disaster warning systems.) When they are identified, they will install time-sensitive triggers keyed to a specific date (perhaps September.) On the designated date, dozens or hundreds of computers would freeze in the middle of vital processes.

HOAXES

It is not necessary to actually use a weapon of mass destruction in order to create terror.
In the days after the World Trade Center bombing, dozens of buildings were evacuated because of fears of another hijacked aircraft. Bomb threats and scares, anonymous threats of plague or chemical attack create high levels of terror at little actual cost to the terrorist. This climate of fear can be as frightening as an actual event.

DANGER LEVEL

Reflects the relative chance that an incident will take place using this WMD in the next five years.

HOMELAND SECURITY

DEFENDING OUR NATION

In May of 2000, George Bush assigned Vice President Dick Cheney with the task of coordinating a national effort to preempt biological, chemical and nuclear threats. At the time, terrorist attacks, even with recent disasters such as the Oklahoma City bombing, seemed a far-off consideration for government officials and citizens alike. But in the days following one of our Nations most devastating invasions of security, the job of combating terrorism has quickly evolved into America's top priority. Correspondingly, the cabinet-level position of Homeland Security, announced by President George Bush in one of our Nations most-watched presidential addresses, has become highly visible.

The idea of the specific term, Homeland Security is recent. In 1997, the term "Homeland Defense" first appeared in a report submitted by the National Defense Panel. In the report titled, *Transforming Defense: National Security in the 21st Century*, the panel anticipates that, "the proliferation of nuclear, chemical and biological weapons and their delivery will pose a serious threat to our homeland and our forces overseas. Information systems, the vital arteries of the modern political, economic and social infrastructure, will undoubtedly be targets as well."

Though concerns such as these have been around for many years, this report first identified "homeland" as a universal term for referring to the protection of American citizens and U.S. government infrastructure. Additional government officials and commissions have referred to this term but the events of September 11 gave new meaning to the notion of "Homeland Security."

Homeland Security, at present, is not clearly defined by our government; no definition of the term exists in the Department of Defense Dictionary of Military and Associated Terms. The Quadrennial Defense Review team

> A position which coordinates the efforts of over 42 departments and agencies in an environment where combatting terrorism has become the most talked about priority in decades is a daunting task. But overwhelming public and government support for action may be what grants the position of Homeland Security an advantage over previous czar-like directorships.

defines it as "prevention, deterrence and preemption of, and defense against, aggression targeted at U.S. territory, sovereignty, population, and infrastructure as well as the management of the consequences of such aggression and other domestic emergencies, civil disturbances, and designated law enforcement efforts."

Many such definitions exist and efforts to generate a governmentally codified term have been introduced by the House of Representatives. Additionally, the United States Commission on National Security, a commission co-chaired by Rudman and Hart, and backed by many in congress, determined in January 2001 that the threats of terrorism against our nation required the creation of a new department combining FEMA, the Customs Service, the Border Patrol and the Coast Guard. Many believed that relative prevention could only be attained by creating a government agency with a substantial budget. However, as recently as four years ago, Republican congress members attempted to eliminate four cabinet departments.

The idea of a Republican White House that would support the creation of a new cabinet department charged with "Homeland Security," was not expected by government insiders. Indeed, President Bush did not generate such a department. Instead Tom Ridge, two term governor of Pennsylvania, was charged with the task of directing a cabinet-level initiative without the support of a department and a corresponding budget. White House aides, however, suggest that Ridge will have access to the budgets of other related agencies.

Tom Ridge will most certainly need to rely on the charisma and initiative that won him the governorship in the heavily democratic state of Pennsylvania if he is to successfully act in concert with the myriad of task forces that have already been working to combat terrorism for decades. But he may need more than that. Many government officials have likened Ridge's position to that of a czar, a leadership position that many citizens and public officials believe will generate dubious results. Notoriously, agencies such as the FBI, the CIA and the U.S. Military as well as their representatives on Capitol Hill have shown resistance to similar positions of oversight in the past. Though the unified climate of the political arena has established a standard of nonpartisan resolve, some government officials have expressed concern surrounding the directorship of "Homeland Security."

A position which coordinates the efforts of over 42 departments and agencies in an environment where combatting terrorism has become the most talked about priority in decades is a daunting task. But overwhelming public and government support for action may be what grants the position of Homeland Security an advantage over previous czar-like directorships. It is conceivable that the same sentiment that joined Democrats and Republicans will assist Ridge in working with previously unresponsive bureaucracies. Moreover, of the many departments charged with the dilemma of dealing with terrorism, none of them are terrorism-specific but instead terrorism is just one of the many items for which they are responsible. This fragmentary sampling of departments and agencies may in fact welcome direction from a leadership source.

The strong friendship, dating back to 1980, between Bush and Ridge may further strengthen the viability of such a position.

Previous czars of drugs and energy causes have oftentimes found that their once highly touted, publicly supported positions have not only fallen out of public interest but that the President, traditionally their primary resource for support, becomes out of reach. A close friendship between George Bush and Tom Ridge may preclude this perpetual failure from occurring in the case of "Homeland Security."

The attack on the World Trade Center and the Pentagon highlighted substantial weaknesses in America's capacity to compile, collect and communicate information about terrorists and potential terrorist activity. The CIA was aware that Khalid Al-Midhar had connections with Bin Laden over 2 years ago. In August of 2000, the agency had enough evidence to put him and an associate on a watch list, but by that time, the two men had already been granted entrance to the country. Before the FBI could locate them, the men had boarded American Flight 77. Airport officials were never provided with their names. Clearly, a great need exists for leadership in the now crucial realm of terrorism. Tom Ridge has both the opportunity and the unique occasion to not only restore America's confidence in government appointed czars but more importantly, he has been called to defend the homeland; a charge for which there has been no greater demand in the history of our nation.

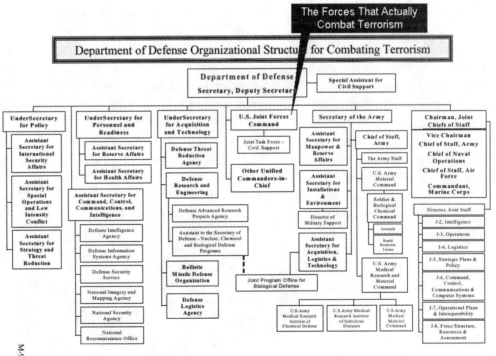

BUILDING COALITIONS

Coalition was the word carefully chosen with very precise meaning to refer to the grand alliance of nations which participated in the Gulf War, and it has been selected again to refer to the new grand alliance against terrorism. Coalition is defined as: A combination, for temporary purposes, of persons, parties, or states, having different and often conflicting interests. The key concepts in the definition are "for temporary purposes" and "conflicting interests."

For Temporary Purposes. The Coalition in the Gulf War was assembled with the explicit understanding that it would continue until its goals were achieved. Coalitions do not always survive until their goals are achieved; many dissolve due to an inability of their members to agree, which prompts the second concept.

Conflicting Interests. Alliances are groups of like-minded people or states. They voluntarily come together because they agree on the value of some group of goals. Coalitions are composed of strange bedfellows: organizations with vastly different goals or philosophies which have agreed to put aside their differences for a specific and well-defined purpose, and who agree that the coalition will, or may dissolve, once that goal has been achieved.

THE GULF WAR COALITION

The Gulf War Coalition was established to liberate Kuwait. By its nature, it consisted of many nations each with disparate interests: many Muslim nations agreed with a goal of liberating Kuwait, but would not have joined if the goal was the destruction of Iraq; some European nations enjoyed trading relationships with Iraq and looked to a future when they could be renewed; the United States considered Iraq a sponsor of international terrorism, and conceivably wanted its government changed to a less belligerent form. All of the members agreed to put aside their divergent interests in order to support a goal on which they all agreed: the liberation of Kuwait.

Once the stated goal of the Gulf War Coalition was achieved --- the liberation of Kuwait --- the pressure for the Coalition to continue evaporated. The United States was not in a position to act alone, and risked negative diplomatic reactions from other members in the Coalition if it did. As a result, the Gulf War ended without decisive action against Iraq. With time, even the punitive and restrictive measures imposed on Iraq after the war were lessened or removed, because the victorious Coalition no longer existed to enforce them.

Building and Maintaining a Coalition. The new Coalition against Terrorism differs greatly from the Gulf War Coalition. Its foundation is a commitment against terrorism "of global reach" (a term carefully crafted to ignore local terrorists and to ensure a palatably common goal for potential members). The new Coalition needs military forces, but most of these will come from the U.S. and a few major allies. The true needs of the Coalition are military bases within range of Afghanistan, overflight permission for air strikes, intelligence sharing, financial sanction enforcement to freeze (and seize) terrorist assets, and perhaps assistance in humanitarian relief operations. At the same time, the coalition building process requires that the leadership of the Coalition not be restricted by too many leaders on the executive committee; a large degree of operational freedom is essential.

The process of coalition building must be undertaken with care. The entry of each new member takes place after a process of negotiation in which the member's agenda and reservations are fully aired; the process itself conveys to the potential member its individual importance in a kind of courting ritual. For example, many Muslim nations do not want Israel to participate (Israel was not allowed to be a member of the Gulf War Coalition; when Iraq attacked Israel with Scuds, the

U.S. was forced to negotiate strongly to keep Israel from retaliating.) Rivalries, competitions, and antipathies between members must be arbitrated or forced into abeyance during the life of the Coalition (India and Pakistan must forego, temporarily, their dispute over Kashmir.)

If you aren't for us, you're against us. Coalitions are ineffective if their mutual goal is so diluted by compromise that it allows no meaningful action. If the new Coalition were solely a military operation, then it would require members with available military forces. Because the contemplated actions of the Coalition range across a broad spectrum of diplomatic, economic, financial, intelligence, and public opinion goals, in addition to military goals, it is possible to recruit members who can make a valuable contribution in one or more of those arenas.

Coalitions have greater credibility than individual states. No one nation-state can simply present its views and expect other states to accept them uncritically. Each state analyzes situations through the lens of self interest. The coalition forming process has already negotiated many different views and needs and distilled them into simple, important, ratified concepts that are more easily accepted by the larger community of nations.

Coalitions create a greater potential for conflict between members. Many potential disputes never blossom into actuality because the potential disputants interact at relatively low levels. When brought together in a coalition, nations must confront their differences as they interact. In addition to high level policy differences, the individual people who are involved on a daily basis risk missteps or misstatements based on simple

cultural differences. President Bush, in calling the War On Terrorism a crusade, used a common word from American culture (Eisenhower's book on World War II was titled *Crusade in Europe*, but one that is charged

---

The military participation in the Gulf War Coalition consisted of: Afghanistan, Argentina, Australia, Bahrain, Bangladesh, Belgium, Canada, Czechoslovakia, Denmark, Egypt, France, Germany, Greece, Hungary, Honduras, Italy, Kuwait, Morocco, The Netherlands, New Zealand, Niger, Norway, Oman, Pakistan, Poland, Portugal, Qatar, Saudi Arabia, Senegal, South Korea, Spain, Syria, Turkey, The United Arab Emirates, The United Kingdom, and the United States.

---

with emotion for Muslims. Bush was quick to apologize and change his wording. Then again, no one has mentioned that the Muslims ultimately won the Crusades.

Coalitions need leadership and management. Coalitions do not form themselves. Their very nature means that a leader must step forward with a vision and the desire to create the coalition. More than that, a coalition

requires continuing management in order for it to stay together. Without management attention, the members drift into inaction and inattention.

HOLDING A COALITION TOGETHER

The divergence of interests among the members of a coalition means there are continuing pressures for individual members to opt out of the coalition. When local opinion within a member nation changes, when elected officials change, or when the international climate changes, the member may reconsider the value of participating in the coalition. The coalition leader must be constantly engaged in conveying to each member the value and positive benefits of past membership and continuing membership. Each members' contribution must be carefully and continually appreciated, at the same time pronouncements must be balanced to avoid offending members who are not mentioned, or who have not as fully participated. Members must also be materially rewarded. The U.S. dropped sanctions against Pakistan in recognition of its entry into the Coalition; having dropped sanctions against Pakistan, the U.S. also had to drop its sanctions against Pakistan's rival India.

THE FAR FUTURE

There will come a point when the Coalition dissolves. At that point, when the postponed disputes and rivalries again become current, the greater potential for the Coalition will be tested. If, during the life of the Coalition, its members have learned to work together for a common purpose, and have conveyed that cooperation to their respective populations, they may be able to continue that spirit of cooperation into resolving some or part of their individual differences.

OUR ALLIES

WHO ARE OUR MOST IMPORTANT ALLIES IN THE WAR ON TERRORISM?

The answer to the question of who will be the United States' most important allies in the war on terrorism must be viewed both from the perspective of who will be helpful in a military campaign in Afghanistan, as well as from the perspective of who will be helpful in coordinating law enforcement and intelligence-gathering activities around the world. Although each of the 60 countries with active Al Qaeda cells will be important on the law enforcement front, a number of states stand out both in their special intelligence capabilities and their abilities to assist in a military campaign. It is important to note that given the unique nature of an operation in Afghanistan, the countries which will be important to the U.S. will be somewhat different from the standards of a normal coalition such as Desert Storm.

EUROPE

NATO - The North American Treaty Organization voted to treat the September 11 attacks on the U.S. as an act of war which triggers NATO treaty obligations. These obligations dictate that if one NATO state is attacked, it is treated as an attack on each NATO state. This will facilitate a coalition military effort, although it will still require consultation to ensure no state feels ignored. NATO states consist of most countries in Western Europe and North America.

United Kingdom - The United Kingdom has always had a 'special relationship' with the United States, and British Prime Minister Tony Blair is ensuring that it continues. The U.K. will be the closest ally of the U.S., and can be counted on for military support of actions in Afghanistan, diplomatic assistance in coalition-building, and law enforcement cooperation at high levels.

France - French President Jacques Chirac was the first world leader to meet with President Bush following the September 11 attacks, and is likely to offer military, diplomatic and law-enforcement assistance to the U.S.

France has its own problems with Islamic militants in its territory, and is eager to cooperate in removing such a threat.

Germany - Germany is also expected to offer military, diplomatic and law-enforcement assistance to the U.S., although it is concerned about the possibilities of the U.S. acting unilaterally, leaving other NATO nations out of the loop, or using foreign intelligence without reciprocating. This is a reminder to the U.S. to consult before acting, and to 'share and share alike' when it comes to law enforcement intelligence.

Russia - President Vladimir Putin's help could be extremely important to the Bush administration and any coalition military response. Russia occupies a strategic location close to Afghanistan, and has influential ties with the former Soviet republics of Tajikistan, Uzbekistan, Kyrgyzstan and Turkmenistan which border or are near Afghanistan. Assistance could come in the form of permitting U.S. forces to use military bases in those republics or in Russia, although military supply lines to such a remote part of the world would be expensive and difficult to initiate. Nevertheless, a joint U.S.-Russian military coalition would be unprecedented, and would benefit from Russian experience in the region.

Furthermore, even if the U.S. decided to use bases in Pakistan, Russian forces could still put pressure on Al Qaeda and Taliban forces from the north in conjunction with the Northern Alliance. Failing that, regional Russian intelligence would greatly assist any U.S. military operations there.

MIDDLE EAST

Israel and the Palestinian Authority - Israel will provide crucial intelligence to U.S. officials for the purpose of rounding up Islamic militants in various parts of the globe, and Palestinian Authority President Yasser Arafat will be important in rallying Arab states to join a coalition against terrorism. Nevertheless, some Arab states may be hesitant to join in military support if it means fighting alongside Israeli forces. As a result, Israeli forces may find themselves sitting on the bench during military operations, as was the case in Operation Desert Storm.

Saudi Arabia and the Gulf States - Saudi Arabia and the United Arab Emirates were two of three states which diplomatically recognized the Taliban government in Afghanistan (the third state is Pakistan). The two demonstrated their commitment to a coalition by severing those ties shortly after the September 11 attacks. Saudi Arabia will be able to assist coalition forces by permitting the use of its airbases for long range operations, although it will have to pay lip service to the more conservative elements in its society which lean towards supporting the Taliban. Many private donations to the Al Qaeda organization originate from this region, and thus, cooperation in restricting this financing will be vital.

Syria - Syria played an important symbolic role when it joined Operation Desert Storm in 1991. Despite its sometimes frosty relations

with the U.S. and its ubiquitous presence on lists of states which sponsor terrorism, Syria joined the effort to expel Iraq from Kuwait and sent a statement about the priorities of the Arab world. Cooperation in this coalition against terrorism would send a similar signal, and would be an important contribution to the global effort.

Egypt - President Hosni Mubarak condemned the September 11 attacks, and has signed up to a general commitment to fight terrorism. Although domestic sentiments are lukewarm, it is questionable to what extent Egypt will be able to offer assistance in a military setting. Nevertheless, the outrage over September 11 may help to achieve more substantive agreement than would have been possible before. Furthermore, Egypt has suffered directly as a result of Al Qaeda-

organized or assisted terrorism, including attempts on the President's life. This will certainly factor significantly in Egypt's decisions regarding what level of involvement it will take.

Jordan - Jordan has been an important ally of the U.S. for decades, and has one of the best intelligence forces in the Middle East. Its assistance in tracing the path of involvement in the September 11 attacks through different cells will be invaluable, as will its intelligence information in a general war on terrorism.

Iran - Iran poses an interesting dilemma for the Bush administration. On one hand, the U.S. has not had any diplomatic relations with Iran since its 1979 fundamentalist Islamic revolution, hostage crisis and subsequent sponsorship of terrorism. Yet on the other hand, the Taliban did not endear itself to Iran when it beheaded a number of Iranian diplomats in

1998. Iran has almost gone to war with the Taliban before, and might be eager to get some kicks in during a coalition effort against the Taliban.

President Muhammed Khatami has been in touch with U.S. officials regarding the coalition, but he is limited in what he can do by conservative religious leaders within his own government. Although it is highly doubtful Iran will go so far as to let the U.S. use its bases or airspace to attack Afghanistan, its policies in the next few years towards the country with which it shares a 580 mile border to the East will have an important effect on the success of any military operations there.

ASIA

Pakistan - As Afghanistan's neighbor to the south, Pakistan may be the United States' most valuable ally in the region, but it must be handled with care. The government of General Pervez Musharraf has offered assistance to the U.S. by granting permission to use its airspace for military strikes and by offering critical local intelligence information regarding Afghanistan. Pakistan may go so far as to permit the U.S. to use its airbases, and to send ground forces into Afghanistan from Pakistan.

Logistically, this would be preferable to launching military operations from inside Central Asia, as supplying forces from the Indian Ocean and neighboring India would be cheaper, faster and easier. Nevertheless, there are serious questions about what such an operation would do to the internal stability of an already fragile country. The one part of the world which is strongly sympathetic to the Taliban outside Afghanistan is northern Pakistan. U.S. forces would

probably find themselves under terrorist attacks before even getting to Afghanistan, and their mere presence in Pakistan could be enough to trigger a widescale rebellion against the Pakistani national government.

India - The Indian government has joined the commitment to fighting global terrorism in full, and has offered significant help to the U.S. in the form of the opportunity to use its territory as a staging ground for any air or land attack on the Taliban regime. Nevertheless, negotiating the acceptance of such an offer will be difficult given the U.S. interest in using Pakistan and the bitter battles between India and Pakistan over the Kashmir region. Like Israel in the Middle East, India may end up not getting taken up on all of its offers for assistance due to the strains it could cause in a coalition which involves its archrival.

China - Handling China presents a dilemma similar (although not as stark) to that of Iran. Although diplomatic relations between the U.S. and China are not warm, China has suffered from terrorism organized by bin Laden's Al Qaeda network in its westernmost provinces, and would be interested in contributing to an end

to that terrorism. U.S. forces in a neighboring country would undoubtedly make China nervous, however, meaning that consultation with China will be essential before proceeding with military action. China does share a small border with Afghanistan, but it is in the Himalayas and would be an impossible location from which to mount a military operation.

Uzbekistan/Tajikistan/Kyrgyzstan - These Central Asian countries have offered assistance to the U.S. and will consider permitting U.S. forces to use their military bases for staging attacks in Afghanistan. Each of these three countries has been ravaged by Islamic terrorism coming from Afghanistan, and each has ethnic populations in Afghanistan which have been 'cleansed' from their homelands in the northern parts of that county.

They already offer assistance to the Northern Alliance forces fighting the Taliban in northern Afghanistan, and are eager to do more to help. But these regions are remote, which means the build-up and supply of forces would probably take more than half a year and billions of dollars. Moreover, these countries are already unstable as a result of small domestic Islamic terror movements, and military forces in the region are barely able to protect themselves from marauding terrorist armies like the IMU. This could present important security concerns for any U.S. or coalition forces operating out of this region.

GATHERING INTELLIGENCE

Intelligence is the foundation for any counter-terrorist activity. Intelligence is defined as analyzed information capable of being used to make well-reasoned decisions about political, diplomatic, legal, or commercial activities. Intelligence is more than simply data or information; it gains its value because it has passed through an analysis process which rates it for reliability and pertinence, and disseminates it to those who need to know about it.

THE INTELLIGENCE CYCLE

Intelligence agencies pursue their mandate to collect intelligence using the Intelligence Cycle, which consists of five steps.

1. Planning and Direction creates the process within the agency and prioritizes various aspects of the effort.

2. Collection acquires information and provides it to the processing system.

3. Processing analyzes the information and converts it into intelligence.

4. Production creates intelligible summaries of the intelligence, reduces it to acceptable formats, warehouses it, and creates retrieval systems such as indexes and catalogs.

5. Dissemination distributes the intelligence to the users.

Unmentioned in the Intelligence Cycle is the fact that some agencies have a continuing interaction with the subjects of their surveillance. They undertake direct action to sabotage the enemy, actively provide incorrect information, and detect enemy agents who are doing the same to them.

THE SOURCES OF RAW INFORMATION

The intelligence community likes to suffix INT to all sorts of sources of information, and a new one seems to appear every year. But the big three of information sources are IMINT (Image Intelligence), SIGINT (Signals Intelligence) and IMINT (Image Intelligence).

IMINT. Images, pictures, photographs, aerial photographs, radar, infra-red, video, and satellite images all belong in the category of Image Intelligence.

SIGINT. Modern electronic equipment produces emissions, or signals, which are categorized as Signals Intelligence. At its simplest, SIGINT listens to radio transmissions. A more complex aspect would be analyzing radar signals in light of current technology to evaluate the capabilities of the equipment.

HUMINT. Human sources of information are called Human Intelligence. This category includes spies and secret agents, but it also includes witnesses, trained observers, and even casual conversations.

No one source of information is supreme. Each has its uses and its failings. In the 1970s, the U.S. shifted away from HUMINT sources, primarily on human rights grounds, but also because a judgment was made that National Technical Means (a euphemism for spy satellites) could handle anything that a HUMINT source could. Somewhat later, the Soviet Union dispatched its latest model fighter to Finland for an air show appearance. The end of the runway was crowded with photographers taking pictures as the aircraft flew by... because satellites can't produce images of the landing gear of aircraft.

THE ANALYSIS PROCESS

Information is useless until it has been processed. Processing involves reviewing the material technically (establishing scale for aerial photographs, decoding encryptions, or translating foreign language information). It also involves correlating new information with old information to determine status changes. Finally, information must be rated for importance. An accurate piece of information, correctly processed to indicate that cars are parked on a street, may still have no importance to any of the issues the intelligence agency is currently considering.

Intelligence Sharing. Some of the information an agency acquires may be developable into intelligence which has no importance to the agency, but great importance to another agency. For example, the FBI was aware of potential terrorists on its watch list, but was slow in sharing that information with the INS. Agencies must share a common perception of priorities if they are to be successful in sharing intelligence.

Classification of Secrets. The United States classifies the level of secrecy for intelligence (and for information before it becomes intelligence) on three levels: Confidential, Secret, and Top Secret. Each higher level reflects an increasing degree of sensitivity. A person with any level of security clearance is permitted to view or access any material with the equivalent security classification or lower. But just because an individual has a Top Secret security clearance, he or she is not automatically allowed to read or access any classified information. Access to classified intelligence is still restricted by a "Need To Know." If the need is not present, access is not granted.

There are also subsets of security classifications. NoForn prohibits access by foreign personnel; Crypto prohibits access by those outside the Cryptography staff, regardless of clearance.

TERRORISM AND INTERNATIONAL LAW

Military force is an appropriate response to some, but not all forms of terrorism. In cases where terrorism suspects live apparently normal lives, blending into communities, law enforcement officers must carry the burden of locating, arresting, and bringing to trial these individuals, no matter where in the world they are living.

This is why international law is important. It provides the mechanism to manage crimes that have international elements and ensure that suspects cannot escape justice. To see how international law can be used to fight terrorism, we should consider first, how international law is used against terrorism today, and second, what the world can do to improve the system we have.

Today, international law deals both with the prevention of terrorism and with the capture and prosecution of accused terrorists. International treaties intend to prevent terrorism by making it more difficult to commit. A good example of this is the 1991 Convention on the Marking of Plastic Explosives for the Purpose of Identification. Created in the aftermath of the bombing of PanAm Flight 103 over Lockerbie, Scotland, this treaty makes it possible for plastic explosives to be detected by electronic scanning equipment in airports. The treaty requires states to make a domestic law which forces explosives manufacturers to treat their explosives with a chemical that is easily identifi

able by baggage screening technology. As a result, it is much more difficult for a potential terrorist to get a bomb onto an airplane successfully in luggage that is left at the check-in desk.

International law can also pave the way for cooperation among states

> In the late 1960s, hijacking civilian airliners became a very popular tactic among terrorists, because they would simply divert the airplane to a sympathetic country with similar ideological views as their own, they would gain much publicity for their cause, and then would be accepted by that country and protected by an offer of political asylum.

in fighting global terrorism. A good example of how this has worked in the past is a series of declarations by the G-7 group of industrialized nations which laid the groundwork for the first intelligence-sharing and substantive cooperative efforts among a group of states in the world on the subject of terrorism. These declarations were later joined by over 100 nations in support of their principles.

But international law also governs cases after an attack has happened, and a terrorist suspect is found in the territory of a foreign country. In the late 1960s, hijacking became a very popular tactic among terrorists, because they would simply divert the airplane to a sympathetic country with similar ideological views as their own, receiving protection in the form of political asylum. But in the 1970s, efforts began to eliminate this type of 'safe haven.' Treaties such as the 1970 Convention for the Suppression of Unlawful Seizure of Aircraft made hijacking an international crime, such that if a hijacker were to fly to a different country, that country would be under a strict obligation either to prosecute him, or to extradite him to a different country for prosecution. Under this formula, in theory, there would be no way for the hijacker to escape prosecution. This hijacking treaty was eventually ratified by over 150 countries, and has entered into 'customary' practice so that it binds every country in the world.

Similar treaties have eliminated safe havens for people who sabotage or bomb airplanes and airports, attack diplomats or state officials, take hostages, improperly use nuclear material, hijack boats, set off bombs, chemical or biological devices or otherwise destroy public places, and finance terrorism. While it has made great improvements in our international system, this legal frame work is not perfect; as we have seen in previous sections of this book, some states still harbor accused terrorists in violation of international law. So how can the system be improved?

First, states are very nervous about sharing intelligence. It involves a great deal of trust, and there is always the possibility that the sensitive information gathered by one country, if shared, could be shared again, end up in the wrong hands, and ruin the original intelligence-gathering initiative. Yet coordinating intelligence and law enforcement activities is the only way to be effective at preventing international terrorist attacks. International legal agreements can establish guidelines which would provide structure and predictability to the way intelligence is used. This is critical if terrorism is to be prevented, since law enforcement and intelligence have to get it right every time, while terrorists only have to get it right once.

Another part of the solution is to strive for more ratification and more consistent enforcement of international anti-terrorism laws. To accomplish this, we must substantially separate law enforcement issues from the world of diplomacy. Today, the decision to extradite an accused international criminal to a country which hopes to prosecute him is often used as a bargaining chip. The country which is harboring the accused may attempt to 'make a deal' which would increase the amount of foreign aid it receives in exchange for the extra

dition of the suspect. In other cases, the country harboring the accused will simply refuse to extradite due to a belief that the accused will not be fairly treated or because it believes the extradition is for political reasons. But if the world can agree to set questions of terrorists' extradition aside from the 'fair' area of negotiations when there is proof of an individual's involvement, a more regular enforcement of the laws would take effect. States which continue to harbor terrorists without prosecuting them should also be punished. For example, when Libya refused to extradite its two government employees who were accused of bombing PanAm Flight 103, punishing sanctions were placed on Libya, compelling it to send the individuals for trial. This type of response should be repeated consistently.

A remaining concern is the way international law prosecutes accused criminals. There is no regular international venue for prosecuting a terrorist. He or she is always prosecuted in a domestic court somewhere. This raises difficult questions about the fairness of a trial. Sometimes states object that extraditing a suspect would give him an unfair trial, while other times, states object that prosecuting a suspect where he is found would give him an unfair trial. In the Lockerbie case mentioned above,

Libya refused to extradite the two suspects immediately, but offered to prosecute them itself. This was rejected by the U.S. and Britain, who believed that two Libyan government employees would automatically be found not guilty. To get around these problems, the U.S. should ratify the International Criminal Court (ICC), and push for the inclusion of terrorism as a crime to be covered by the court.

In 1998, an international convention assembled the basic design of an international criminal court which could hear cases from around the world involving war crimes and crimes against humanity. This court will come into existence once sixty countries have ratified the treaty. The U.S. refuses to ratify it due to concerns that it could become abusive and unfairly prosecute U.S. citizens for international crimes. But it seems clear that this institution would actually be one step removed from international politics, and would facilitate the disposition of international criminal law in a way that the U.S. is desperate to see happen. From this book's discussion of the definition of terrorism earlier, there can be no question that the features which make terrorism an international crime qualify it to be heard in front of an international tribunal such as the ICC. In fact, due to the political rancor associated with certain terrorism cases, the added element of impartiality, were it to be widely perceived, would make terrorism a perfect crime to be tried there.

THE MONEY TRAIL

The science of economics deals with choices based on limited resources. The common currency for such resources is money, and without money nothing can happen. Everything is driven by economics. The grandest of political plans remains only a dream if money is not allocated to accomplish it. The most profound of religious revelations cannot be disseminated without the donations of money to support its evangelists. Even the simplest of terrorist schemes cannot be implemented unless its culprits have the money to support them and to buy their weapons or explosives.

THE SOURCES OF MONEY

The need for money by Afghan based terrorists has lead them to four basic sources: the drug trade, charitable contributions, personal assets (including continuing income from investments and business), and speculative investments.

NARCO-TERRORISM. TERRORISM FINANCED BY DRUG OPERATIONS.

CONTRIBUTION

HIGH

There are two mirror image definitions of narco-terrorism. Terrorism conducted to further the aims of drug traffickers. Violence to disrupt legitimate government to divert attention from drug operations.

While they are not mutually exclusive, the two definitions confirm the truism that terrorism needs money in order to exist, and drug production and distribution are a relatively easy source of large amounts of money outside the traditional economic system.

Afghanistan is the world's largest producer of opium, with year 2000 production estimated at 3275 tons. The Taliban controlled 96% of the territory under opium cultivation in 2000. In mid-2000, the Taliban banned opium cultivation (ostensibly to eliminate the drug trade) and was

> Afghanistan is the world's largest producer of opium, with year 2000 production estimated at 3275 tons. The Taliban controlled 96% of the territory under opium cultivation in 2000. ...Taliban supreme leader Mullah Omar has stated, "The use of opium is wrong, but the selling is not wrong according to Islamic law."

originally applauded for its action. More recent United Nations statements have questioned why the Taliban has not destroyed existing stockpiles, saying that the Taliban is the major beneficiary of drug sales. Before the cultivation ban, 1 kilo of opium sold for $35; its current price is as much as $360. The current interpretation is that the cultivation ban was intended to overcome an opium oversupply and to increase prices.

Taliban supreme leader Mullah Omar has stated, "The use of opium is wrong, but the selling is not wrong according to Islamic law." In reality, Islam forbids both the use of and selling of any type of illegal drugs, including opium, using the same logic that forbids the free mixing of the sexes because it can lead to sexual immorality.

The Kyrgyzstan Security Council, for instance believe the military operations of terrorist groups in southern Central Asia are designed to protect drug routes from the state authorities. In addition, some Islamic terrorist organizations have resorted to criminal terrorism in order to finance their activities, including kidnappings and robberies.

Charitable Contributions. The desperate conditions in Afghanistan, wracked by war and drought, have brought massive

CONTRIBUTION MODERATE

amounts of humanitarian aid to that nation. But the limitations on foreign aid and UN relief workers by the Taliban have exposed many of them to restrictions and harassment, and virtually all of them have been withdrawn from the country. Some of the gap has been filled with Muslim charities providing free or subsidized bread and other food.

These Muslim charities are funded by contributions, primarily from faithful Muslims around the world, fulfilling one of the pillars of their faith: to provide for the poor.

As UN and western relief agencies withdraw from Afghanistan, Muslim charities are being recruited to fill the void. In an environment hospitable to terrorist organizations, these charities represent an opportunity for direct or indirect support of those terrorists.

In addition, the Saudi Arabian government is the single largest supporter of Islamic relief organizations around the world. While much of this charity is spent on actual relief operations, many of these relief organizations have "miscellaneous" or undocumented projects, some of which are reported to be terrorist organizations.

Personal Assets. Osama bin Laden is reported to have a personal fortune in excess of $270 million. Personal **CONTRIBUTION LOW** wealth, however, is rarely totally liquid; it includes the value of real estate, personal property, and investments in businesses and stocks. Investments produce an income stream return which is the source of day to day living expenses, and of money to support terrorist activities.

Osama bin Liden is not the only financial supporter of Islamic fundamentalist terrorism. Wealthy individuals throughout the world, recruited over time through appeals to religious responsibility and through personal contact, continue to provide financial support.

Speculation. Financial speculation succeeds best when the speculator knows **CONTRIBUTION LOW** or strongly believes he knows what the future holds. The degree of unfairness this represents is why stock markets ban insider trading. And the ultimate insider trading occurs when the speculator plans a disaster and knows when it will take place. Unusual levels of speculation in airline stocks immediately prior to the World Trade Center bombings

immediately raised suspicions that the terrorists made efforts to profit from their actions through the selling.

TRACING MONEY

The United States has long worked to freeze terrorist assets in the United States and to enforce sanctions against the Taliban and Afghanistan. Those actions are part of the reason for the Taliban's embracing of drug sales: which is the only avenue for large scale financial support. U.S. efforts were restricted because they were unable to trace or freeze foreign accounts.

The World Trade Center attack, however, allowed the U.S. to insist on cooperation from foreign governments and foreign banks. Using a carrot and stick approach, the U.S. has enlisted nations in the new Coalition. While affirming that everyone benefits by condemning terrorism, the U.S. threatened sanctions for failure to cooperate in financial transaction tracing and asset freezes.

Banking and Investment Transactions. Most financial transactions in the West are impersonal accounting transfers with audit trails which can be traced. Wire transfers, money orders, even travelers checks can be traced to companies or individuals. With cooperation from foreign banks, it is possible to trace the flow of money to individuals who can be interviewed and even detained or prosecuted. In addition to providing evidence of individuals involved with terrorism or support of terrorism, the process of following the money trail serves as a strong deterrent to future transactions, with a consequent drying up of financial support.

Cash Transactions. Western drug operations rely strongly on cash transactions. The U.S. has no $1,000 notes in circulation primarily because

they would aid drug dealers in transferring large amounts of money. Drug dealers often resort to weighing their cash instead of counting it because of the tedium and time required to make an accurate hand count. Terrorists (especially narco-terrorists) with large organizations require large sums of money to finance the basic living and overhead expenses of their organizations.

Cash transactions are naturally restricted because of their bulk; a package of a million dollars, for example, weighs hundreds of pounds. There are informal cash transfer methods in place. For example, the Halawa system transfers money based on trust and relationships rather than formal documents. These cash transfer systems, however, cannot efficiently handle frequent transactions in large amounts.

One proposal for the military is that its Special Operations Forces target drug operations in Afghanistan and neighboring central Asia to destroy stockpiles of drugs and cash.

THE GLOBALIZATION OF COOPERATION

The creation of the Coalition against Terrorism has mandated cooperation between nations for financial intelligence sharing and financial seizures, which is the only effective counter to the growing globalization of terrorist networks.

CONCLUDING THOUGHTS

THE BALANCING ACT: CIVIL LIBERTIES VS. NATIONAL SECURITY

On September 26, thousands of New York citizens idled in their cars for hours as New York police conducted random vehicle searches. Every driver, thwarted from meeting deadlines or returning home, when interviewed, patiently uttered unilateral support for the searches. In the climate of post-disaster fall-out, Americans have exhibited phenomenal unity, commitment, and benevolence. Giving blood and donating money doesn't seem sufficient, and so, when federal officials, police and local leaders implore citizens to endure random searches, wire taps, and internet surveillance, Americans are all too willing to comply.

Thurgood Marshall, in Skinner v. Railway Labor Executives said that "History teaches that grave threats to liberty often come in times of urgency, when constitutional rights seem too extravagant to endure." Americans, New Yorkers and foreign nationals, those of us who escaped personal loss on September 11, feel that to speak out against inconveniences and potential threats to our civil liberties is synonymous with such aforementioned extravagance; how can we possibly dissent and defend our own needs when our friends and neighbors are suffering so deeply? But it is precisely this pure, untarnished sentiment that renders us vulnerable to the erosion of all that is dear to us: our America, our freedom, our civil liberties.

Capitol Hill feels the same unity, the altruistic need to sacrifice. But leaders are also compelled to protect us. It is their elected responsibility to make sure that our children are well taught, our drinking water is safe from pollutants and that we are liberated from the horrors of terrorism. It is not intrinsic hankering for

> "History teaches that grave threats to liberty often come in times of urgency, when constitutional rights seem too extravagant to endure."
> --*Thurgood Marshall*

dictatorship that moves politicians to lower the threshold of probable cause and loosen the control on wiretapping authority. Similarly, it is not the public's desire to shrug off America's coveted civil liberties by acquiescing to more liberal FBI on-line monitoring, monitoring to which many were previously, avidly opposed.

Herein lies the danger. Our teachers, parents and spiritual leaders have always urged us to look to the heart of the matter. To examine the spirit of an act when searching for its truth. And the spirit of America has never been more pure. Indeed, if our motivations are good, how is it possible that our actions might threaten our freedom? Perhaps it is because

we must look to the hearts of others to garner understanding. Rather than blame politicians for limiting our civil rights, rather than criticizing the public for complying with those limitations, we should take a long, comprehensive, unwavering look into the hearts of the men who masterminded and coordinated these attacks.

The Terrorists. They are the people who caused this, they are the people who conceived of it, these are the hearts that need examining. Many contend that the heart of a terrorist is absent of critical elements, vital for normal, emotional functioning. But to dismiss such individuals as evil is too simple and does not lead us to greater understanding. Simply put, terrorists seek to control, to restrict, to frighten. In most definitions of terrorism, political agenda is a significant factor. The September 11th attacks were undoubtedly political; political statements from totalitarian organizations that inflict some of our world's most despicable civil rights abuses on their own people. The terrorists want us to stop concerning ourselves with the rights of these nations and so they employed the same, method of intimidation that they use on their own citizens.

Here we see a significant Civil Liberties dilemma: Is it America's right to defend the civil liberties of individuals that do not fall under the purview of our constitution? Is a woman, forced to live in poverty with no prospects for employment our humanitarian concern or simply the business of the state in which she resides? Are children, raised to believe that death in war is of the highest calling, brainwashed and victimized, or students of a faith that the rest of us don't understand and don't have the right to judge? Is America undermining our commitment to freedom of speech and religion by interfering with other countries, other ideas, different religions? Or is America truly the leading moral authority, called to protect those who are weak and suffering? Many believe that it is.

And if America decides that defending the freedom of others is indeed the business of our Nation, as it has many times in its history, it is paramount that we preserve and protect the civil liberties of our own people first and foremost; because if our civil liberties become corrupted, we can no longer share them with others. The terrorists have subjected us to unspeakable harm. They have frightened us, intimidated us and

compelled some of us to behave with unforgivable bigotry. We must protect ourselves not just from bodily harm, the sadness of loss and economic instability, but from liberal arrest policies, racial profiling, and the willingness of citizens to give up the very freedoms that make America great.

In 1974, The Irish Republican Army bombed a pub in Great Britain. In short order, the government introduced the Prevention of Terrorism Temporary Provisions Bill that permits suspected terrorists to be searched without warrant, prohibits individuals from wearing clothes that may support such an organization and makes speech that supports the sentiments of terrorist groups, broadcast on radio or television, illegal. Wire taps are done without judicial approval and in Northern Ireland, coerced confessions obtained by police brutality are admitted as evidence. But many residents are pleased with the new measures and argue that increased surveillance and specific free speech restrictions do not affect the majority of law-abiding citizens. They feel secure.

And it is clear that Americans do not. Our care-free way of living has been muted and many live in fear. Further provisions, such as sky marshalls, improved surveillance, better security at airports and improved intelligence gathering are all necessary if we are to move forward with confidence. Without such basic security measures, our civil liberties become useless, stifled by fear and reserve.

Benjamin Franklin once said that "people who trade their fundamental liberty for a little temporary security deserve neither." But Americans deserve both. We have been brave, heroic, unified and proud. And we are entitled. We deserve safety in our country, but we must not sacrifice our "sweet land of liberty" in a mad dash for cover. Americans and politicians must closely examine newly proposed safety measures. Such measures are vital to our well being. But before rushing to back them in a blind show of emotional support, we must examine such measures carefully so that the very restrictions that we hope will protect us do not corrode the liberal exchange of ideas and the ethnic diversity that are integral to the foundation of this country. Because these are the very things that the terrorists sought to take away from us. And in the name of the thousands who died, we must not relent.

AFTERWARD

The terrorist attacks on the U.S. on September 11, 2001 were profoundly shocking to the nation due to their scale, their targets, their callous disregard for innocent life, and the simple fact that they took place on the soil of our mainland. Hopefully, this book has offered a brief background and context to those attacks which will make it easier to understand both why we were attacked, and what we can do to try to prevent it from happening again. But people are still wondering: what can I do? After giving blood and donating money, the average person is still left feeling vaguely helpless, wanting to make himself or herself useful, wondering what else can be done.

One answer is to stay engaged. Important choices will continue to present themselves over the long term, and our nation will need to reflect seriously on our priorities and values, both internationally and domestically. This reflection will take place not in the corridors of power, but in the hearts of individuals.

On an international level, it is important that American citizens remain vigilant and informed. Sections of this book have weighed the possibilities of military action in Afghanistan, but in the long term, we will be faced with the question of what to do with a country which has a broken economy, little infrastructure and even less hope. A country in an area which will always be a recruiting ground for the disenchanted and the desperate unless fundamental changes occur in the conditions of life in the region. It will be our duty as citizens to think about, discuss and decide how we should treat complicated problems such as this, and how we as a nation want to present ourselves to the world.

But we will also be faced with important decisions in our own land. The twinge of paranoia that may result from the sense of vulnerability engendered by these attacks has the potential to lead us down a dangerous path. The specter of racial profiling, which treats fellow citizens as suspected criminals simply due to their appearance, is but one pernicious example of a response borne of fear. We must try not to lose the revitalized community spirit which has sprung up to fill the void left in our hearts. We must engage with our communities, ensure their vitality, and ensure that we do not set upon each other as the result of a horrible disaster. If we fail in this task, the terrorists will already have won.